S0-ECX-796

The Amazon

Library of Congress Number: 88-18337

2 3 4 5 6 7 8 9 0 97 96 95 94 93 92

Library of Congress Cataloging-in-Publication Data

Dorst, Jean, 1924-
[Amazzonia. English]
The Amazon / Jean Dorst.

— (World nature encyclopedia)
Translation of: Amazzonia
Includes index.
Summary: Describes the geographic features, climate, and plants and animals of the Amazon River region with emphasis on their interrelationship.
1. Ecology—Amazon River Region—Juvenile literature. 2. Biotic communities—Amazon River Region—Juvenile literature. [1. Ecology—Amazon River Region. 2. Biotic communities—Amazon River Region. 3. Amazon River Region.] I. Title. II. Series: Natura nel mondo. English.
QH112.D6713 1988 574.5'.0981'1—dc19 88-18368
ISBN 0-8172-3325-3

WORLD NATURE ENCYCLOPEDIA

The Amazon

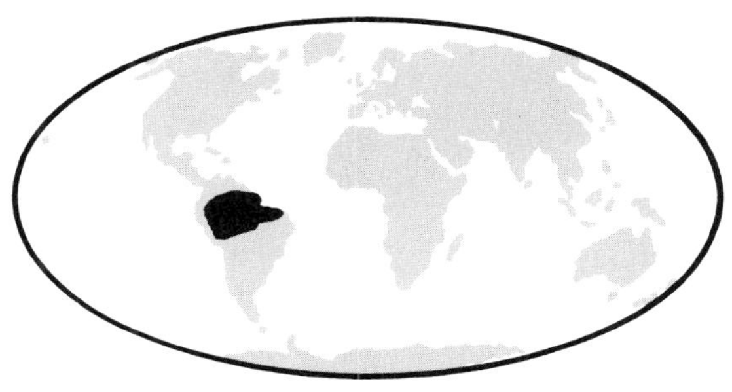

Jean Dorst

RAINTREE
STECK-VAUGHN
LIBRARY
Austin, Texas

CONTENTS

INTRODUCTION

"All of a sudden I found myself in a new world, far from any civilization, upon a sea of fresh water, in the center of a maze of lakes, rivers, and canals—an intricate network that penetrates, from every direction, an immense forest to which water is the only possible access." These were the words of Charles-Marie de La Condamine as he sailed down the Amazon River in 1743.

A century later Henry Walter Bates and his friend Alfred Russel Wallace arrived in the Amazon after crossing the Atlantic Ocean from England. "It is with great emotion," he wrote, "that my friend and I, both in a tropical country for the first time, encounter these lands.... To the west, through the captain's telescope, we see a long stretch of forest emerging from the water—a mass so thick it is hard to distinguish the individual trees. This is the boundary of a huge forest which holds many wonders in its most secret corners and cloaks the continent in green for millions of miles, from our point of landing to the foothills of the Andes."

A traveler in modern times would reach the Amazon by air. Certainly it is, today, a more comfortable experience than the explorers of the past had. The wonder and amazement of such a journey, however, would be unchanged. The

modern visitor would fly over vast forests that create a broad, leafy canopy. This canopy is broken up only by ribbons of black and yellow water. These are some of the streams that flow into the world's largest river, the Amazon. Its basin occupies two-fifths of South America.

The visitor would discover a wondrous environment made up of rivers and forests. At first, each stream or patch of trees seems very much the same. In fact, each differs greatly. This broad area extends across the entire basin as far as Guyana. It is an amphibious universe of trees, water, sun, and fierce heat. To some, it can be a frightening universe of gigantic spiders, snakes, and disease-carrying insects. But it is also a marvelous universe. Teeming with over two million species of plants and animals, the Amazon is home to a greater variety of living things than any other environment on earth.

The Amazonian forest never seems to change. In spite of recent geological events, it is a haven for many species and, simultaneously, a place where new life forms continue to develop. It is also a "green hell," where a person can become lost and even starve to death among fantastic animals and plants.

GEOLOGICAL HISTORY AND CLIMATE

Preceding pages: *Forests and Indian dwellings are mirrored by a river in the Amazon.*

Opposite page: As far as the eye can see lies the Amazon forest. In the large Amazonian or Guyanese cities, the tourist is offered excursions into the "virgin forest" to see its animals and to visit the Indians who live according to the customs of their ancestors. Those who go along will not see much of the real Amazon, neither its primitive flora and fauna, nor its Indians. When the tourists leave the small "typical" village, where they have spent some of their dollars, the inhabitants will put their farmers' clothes back on and go back to work. The Amazon remains a hard country, difficult to penetrate without economic sacrifice and assured discomfort.

A single glance at a map of South America is enough to locate the Amazon Basin. It covers over 2.7 million square miles (7 million square kilometers). The greater part of this territory belongs to Brazil, but it also includes the eastern provinces of Venezuela, Colombia, Ecuador, Peru, and Bolivia. In the face of the giant river, all smaller ones appear insignificant.

A Story Both Ancient and New

The history of the Amazon is ancient, dating back to the earliest times known to geologists. That part of the planet is situated on an enormous depression in the center of an ancient Precambrian shield, which is a major structural unit of the earth's crust formed more than 600 million years ago. To the north, this shield surfaces in the Guyana Highlands. To the south, it appears on the Brazilian plateau. Both of these formations are made up of rugged, crystalline rocks that underwent changes over time due to heat, pressure, and chemical activity.

The Amazonian depression has been filled during the course of time by sediment from both the sea and the continent. The most ancient known deposits date from the Cambrian period, 500 million years ago. The earliest fossils found belong to the Silurian period. These can be dated to around 400 million years ago. From those remote times through relatively recent geological periods, the Amazon Basin drained into the Pacific Ocean.That is, it flowed west and not east, as it does today. Only in the Cretaceous period (120 million years ago) did land, which would later become the easternmost part of the basin, begin to discharge its waters into the Atlantic Ocean.

At that time, the Atlantic was becoming larger. This was due to the detachment and drift of the American continent from the African continent. The central and western parts of the region were occupied by a vast Pacific gulf. They formed a group of valleys open to the west. This geographic configuration was maintained throughout the Tertiary period while sedimentation continued.

During the Miocene epoch, fifteen million years ago, an event occurred that profoundly modified the South American continent. The Andes chain rose up at the site of a gigantic geosyncline. A geosyncline is a great downward flexure, or fold, of the earth's crust. This was caused by pressure from a shifting Pacific plate. Instead of pouring into the Pacific, the waters of the basin formed a huge lake

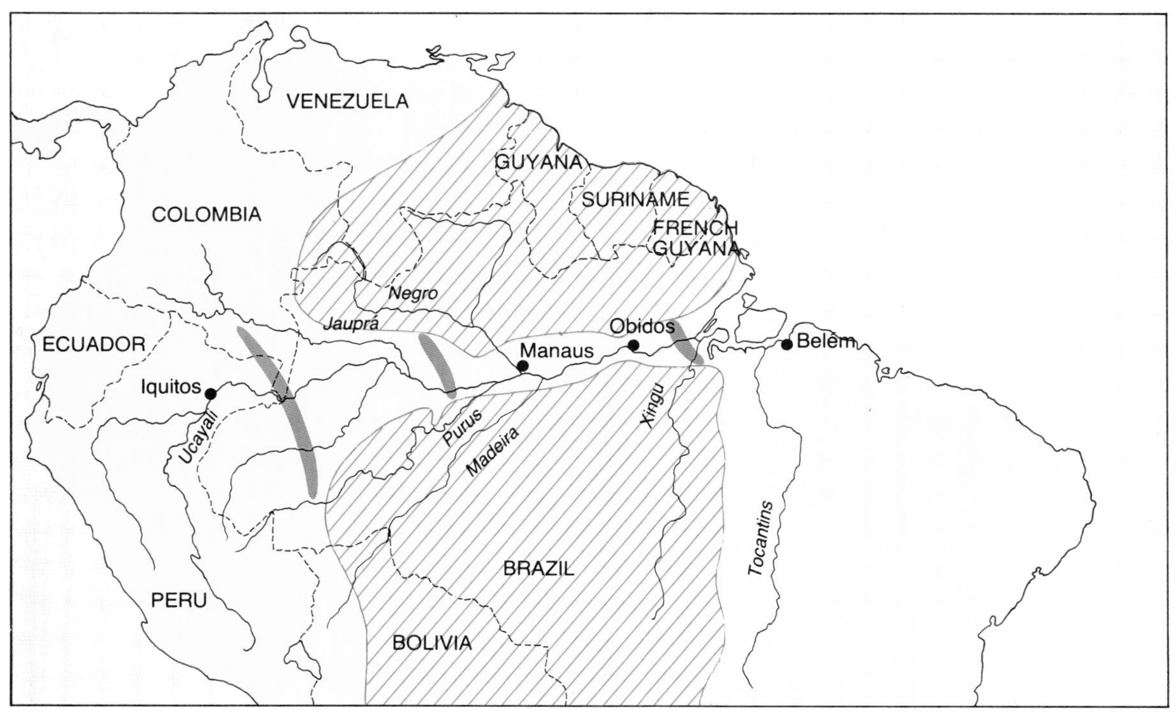

Formed of very ancient crystalline rock, the Guyanese and Brazilian shields (areas diagonally shaded) reach both sides of the Amazon River Valley. Following the rise of the Andes, the waters of the great future river forced an opening between these two masses and the secondary sediments deposited at their margins. The valleys of the Amazon River and of the lower reaches of its tributaries have been filled by rather recent deposits of sediment. Three ridges (areas indicated in orange), or arcs, divided the Amazon into smaller basins before vanishing beneath the mass of sediments carried by the rivers.

surrounded by marshes. Later, new sediment was added in thick layers. These layers are visible today in outcroppings in Peru, Ecuador, and Columbia. Only when the waters carved an opening toward the east between the Guyana Highlands and the Brazilian plateau was the present Amazonian plane formed. Evidence of the opening of this waterway can be found in the region near Mount Alegre in Brazil. There, several small hills beside the riverbed are all that remain of the ancient barrier.

The sedimentation, or the action of depositing sediment, continued. The Andes, which had reached a considerable height by this time underwent significant erosion. The rivers that flowed toward the east (most of those that crossed what is now Ecuador and Peru) began to cut into the mountains. This created deep valleys and canyons. As new sediment was distributed throughout the plain, some localities developed very high layers. This phenomenon continued for the entire Quaternary period. During this time a succession of alternately humid and dry, cold and hot periods repeatedly modified the mix of ocean and fresh water. Even today, this action continues and can be seen by the volume of sediment carried in the rivers. The Amazon River, which collects all of the waters of the immense basin, carries a great mass of detritus, minerals or bits of rock derived from the weathering of existing rock, into the Atlantic Ocean. It passes through an estuary, a water passage where a river current meets the tide, 186 miles (300 km) wide. The result is an enormous cone-shaped deposit through which the current, coursing to the open sea, has carved a deep underwater canyon. Some of the sediment that reaches the sea is pushed along by strong northerly currents that extend from Brazil all the way to the coast of Guyana. Because of these currents, a true delta has never formed at the mouth of the Amazon River.

Today, the Amazon Basin covers a vast plane. The slightest differences in altitude, caused by sedimentation and the destructive or constructive forces of water, affects the various types of vegetation. Spreading open like a large fan toward the west, as if to collect the largest possible quantity of water, the Amazon Basin narrows in the east. Near Obidos, and before it broadens into an immense mouth, the river is reduced to a few miles in width. The basin has been compared to a gigantic saucer. It is a slightly

Pictured is a spectacular aerial view of the tropical Amazonian forest, cut by a large, sinuous river and its tributaries. The Amazon Basin covers 2,722,000 square miles (7,050,000 sq. km). The land is relatively flat yet very nearly impenetrable. It is impossible to travel more than 3 miles (5 km) in a straight line without encountering a stream of water that must be forded before proceeding through the tangle of vegetation.

An aerial view of the Amazon forest shows the thick fog that often envelops it for vast stretches. Land and water are profoundly linked in this great basin.

exaggerated image, but it does give a fairly accurate impression.

The plateaus of Guyana and Brazil have an entirely different geomorphological nature. ("Geomorphology" is the study of the land and the underwater features of the earth's surface.) From a geological point of view, they can be considered part of the Amazon Basin. The altitudes are high but not exceptional. For example, the mountains of Tumuc Humac in northeastern Brazil, barely reach 2,625 feet (800 meters). Along the borders of Venezuela, Guyana, and Brazil are ancient sandstone "massifs," principal mountain masses, reaching 9,187 feet (2,800 m). Although this region is not actually in the Amazon Basin, spurs of tropical river forest push deep into the heart of these mountains. It is a reminder of the tenacity of that type of vegetation.

An Isolated Continent

In order to explain the uniqueness of South America's flora and fauna, and particularly that of Amazonia, it is necessary to look at the geological history of the area. Two hundred million years ago, the continent was still united with Africa. Studies have shown that the ancient mountain chains and rock strata (layers) on both sides of the Atlantic Ocean show remarkable similarities. In addition, there is a common biological base shared by the two sites. After the separation of the two continents, two distinct and separate evolutionary lines originated from this foundation.

The two continents started separating 135 million years ago. The resulting fissure has been growing continuously ever since. In this way, the Atlantic Ocean was born. For a long time, South America remained isolated from the rest of the world. It was even disconnected from North America, which was closer to Europe and Asia. In a sense, South America's situation then bore certain similarities to that of Australia today. Isolation allowed the continent to develop an incredible number of native species, genera, and even families of plants and animals. Evolution on the South American continent is expressed in a unique way. In many groups of living organisms, the species are barely distinguishable from each other. It appears as if they had just begun to diverge. Moreover, the variety of natural environments has favored an abundance of species. Each one is well adapted to its own ecological niche, or biological and physical space occupied by a species. This is especially true in the Amazon region.

In relatively recent geological times, a continental bridge between South and North America was formed. It is known today as Central America. This development proved favorable to potentially migratory species. In comparison, in Europe, Africa, and Asia, the presence of the Mediterranean Sea and the African desert formed an effective barrier against the northward migration of species typical of tropical areas.

Very few species have migrated from the north to Central and South America. This is particularly true of mammals. Only monkeys, bats, and rodents are numerous in South America, and these evolved from very ancient native species. Many groups of mammals are completely absent or play a minor role in the animal communities.

South America, in general, and the Amazon Basin, in particular, are characterized by the originality of some spe-

Below: This graph shows yearly rainfall is evenly distributed throughout the Amazon Basin. The shape and height of the curves represent the variations in monthly precipitation from January through December. The abundance of rain throughout most of the year in the northeastern Amazon regions is apparent. There is a marked peak at the Brazil-Guyana border. In the southern parts of the Amazon, a more-or-less defined humid season coincides with the winter. These differences are caused by the change of the sun's position in the sky on either side of the equator, as well as by the exposure of the basin to the major eastern winds. These winds release their rain first on the Atlantic regions of the Amazon and then on the huge Andes chain that finally stops them.

Opposite page: On the graph are variations in yearly rainfall throughout the Amazon Basin. In Iuarete (1), rainfall is plentiful all year long. The same is true of Belém (2), where maximums occur during winter and spring in the Northern Hemisphere.

cies. They are also noted for absence of other species that are very common all around the world. Interestingly enough, marsupials, which do not live in other parts of the world, are found in South America and Australia. This fact is used as evidence of the existence, a long time ago, of a vast continent linking the southern part of the Americas to Australia and the Antarctic region.

A Hot, Humid Climate

The Amazon Basin is well known for its hot and humid climate throughout the entire year. This is easily explained by its geographical position. The equator cuts it in half, so the length of the day is fairly constant. Fluctuations are no greater than an hour either way. The sun heats up the atmosphere throughout the year, even though clouds may often filter or block its rays. In Manaus in the western part of Brazil, the average exposure to the sun does not exceed eight hours a day in August. In December, it is about four hours a day, and the sky is 70 to 85 percent covered by clouds. In spite of this, the heating power of the sun is always very high. The monthly average temperature in Manaus throughout the year varies between 78° Fahrenheit

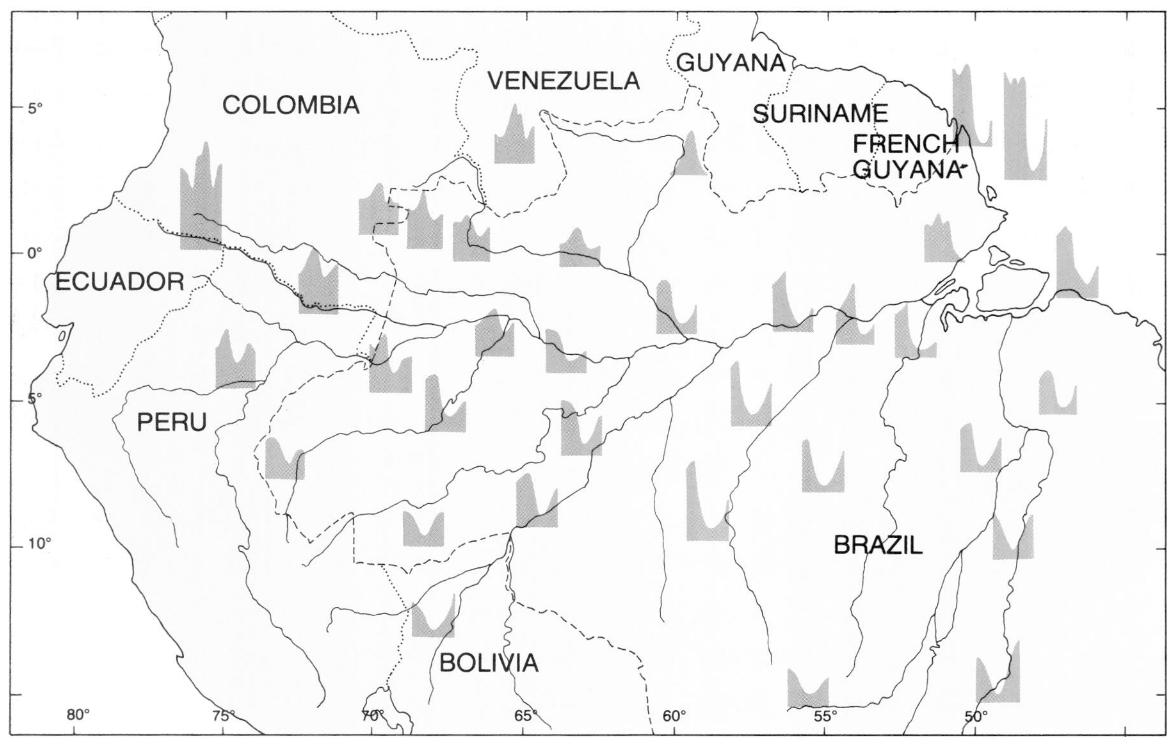

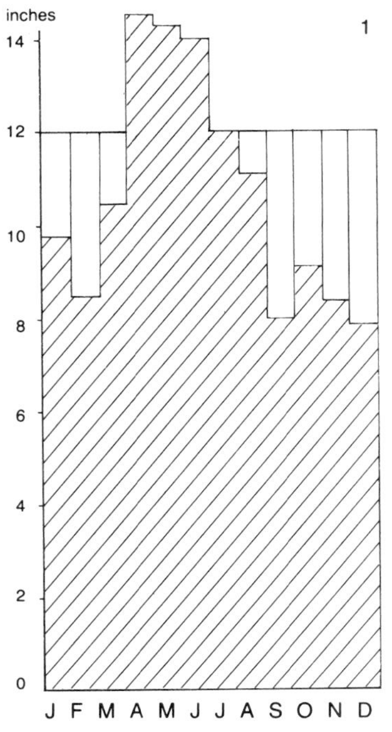

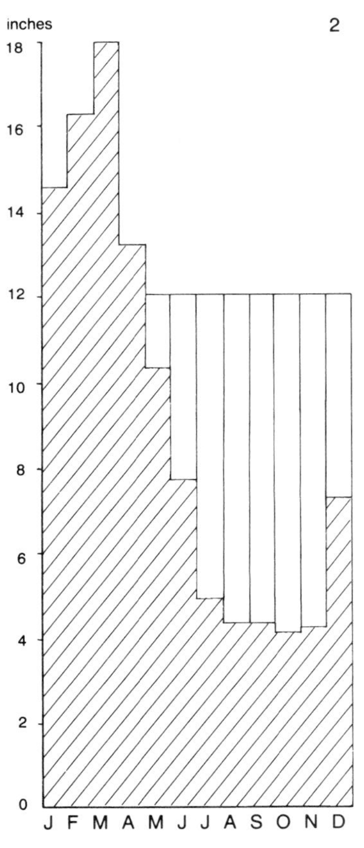

(25.6° Celsius) in March and April and 82°F (27.8°C) in September and October. The extreme high and low temperatures, however, may differ much more. For example, during December the temperature can rise to between 93° and 104°F (34° and 40°C). In July and August at dawn, the thermometer can drop to as low as 48°F (9°).

The second important climatic factor is the abundance of rain. The atmosphere is always very humid, and the yearly rainfall in the Amazon is as high as 90 inches (2,300 millimeters). For comparison, in Rome, Italy, 29 inches (744 mm) of rain fall annually. In Paris, France, 24 inches (619 mm) of rain fall. The quantity of rainfall is substantially greater in the eastern part of the basin. Near Amap , it is 140 inches (3,600 mm) annually. It diminishes in the center at Manaus to 86 inches (2,200 mm) and climbs again toward the west where the great Andes chain traps the clouds. This is not far from the intensely humid northwestern regions of Colombia, which receive 315 inches (8,000 mm) of rainfall per year. This extremely high precipitation makes the region one of the wettest on the planet.

Rain comes from the direction of the Atlantic Ocean and is carried by the trade winds. The eastern areas, therefore, are the first to receive it. One-fourth of the rain that falls on the Amazon forests is retained by the leaves and never touches the ground. A second amount is reabsorbed into the atmosphere from plants through the processes of evaporation and transpiration. This amounts to a considerable quantity of water vapor, which eventually forms new clouds. Its volume is comparable to the volume of water vapor carried from the sea by the trade winds. This supports a belief held by some biologists. A forest as wide as the Amazon is, in effect, equivalent to the gulf of a sea as far as facilitating the cycling of water between the earth and atmosphere is concerned.

The yearly rainfall at a given location is important, but equally significant is the seasonal distribution of the rainfall. In the Amazon, it rains practically all year. Thus the forest is always green. However, during summer in North America, rainfall in South America is markedly lower on the eastern part of the Amazon Basin. This is because the sun is over the northern hemisphere.

Dry Savannas in the Heart of the Amazon

The huge Amazon forest is interrupted now and then by prairies that are either grassy or covered by delicate

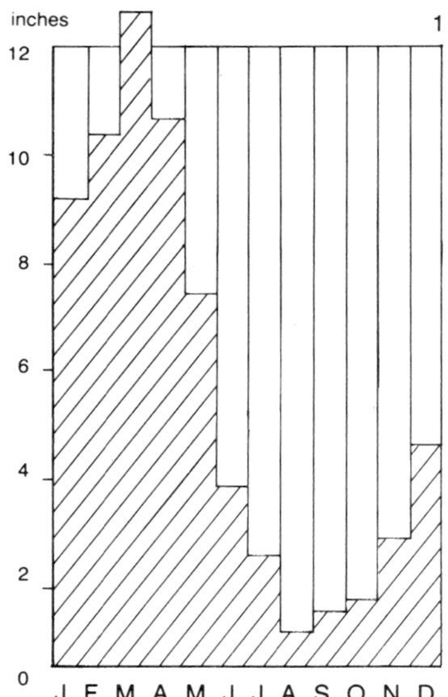

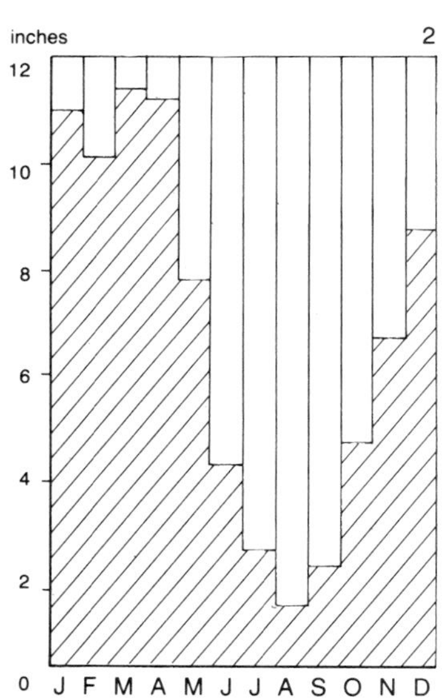

The graph shows yearly variations in rainfall throughout the Amazon Basin at Obidos (1) and Manaus (2), located to the west of laurete and Belém. During summer in the Northern Hemisphere. Obidos and Manaus are relatively dry, although some rain does fall.

bushes. This phenomenon is especially common in the higher region of the Branco River basin. There, the rainfall is relatively plentiful, but it is unevenly distributed throughout the year. The periodic droughts, together with the high permeability (the quality of being penetrable) of the sandy soils, do not permit the growth of a permanent forest on this land.

An Unchanging Climate

The climate has remained largely unchanged throughout the Amazon Basin since the Tertiary period, ten million years ago. High temperatures and humidity prevail. These conditions have enabled some organisms that evolved in ancient times to survive unchanged throughout the geological eras. As living fossils still so well adapted to their ecological niches, they offer strong evidence for evolution. Examples from the birds include the hoatzin (crested, olive colored, and smaller than a pheasant) and the trogon (a large family of various nonsong birds with brilliant plumage). The marsupials among the mammals and a variety of insects are also good examples. However, the stability of the climate cannot explain the enormous diversity of flora and fauna in this region. This diversity is primarily due to climatic changes that took place in some areas. They have affected some regions since the end of the Tertiary period and also during the Pleistocene epoch. The Pleistocene is the epoch when contemporary populations developed.

It has been known for some time that the great glaciations profoundly modified the climate of the northern hemisphere by covering vast areas with ice. Naturally, this did not occur in tropical areas.

Both geologists and biologists agree that the Amazon is not excluded from these fluctuations. The forest cover was repeatedly subdivided into large green "islands" widely separated from each other by grassy prairies. In the analysis of modern soils, traces of this phenomenon that affected the Amazon through the Pleistocene epoch can be found. Today, it is still possible to recognize some of these islands. They are characterized by a higher-than-average rainfall and the presence of plants and animals absent elsewhere. The experts do not always agree about the location of these islands, but all do agree that they exist.

During the driest periods, both the plants and the animals found safe refuge in the forests. Each time a plant or animal species found itself isolated in a separate population, it evolved in a slightly different way. This produced new forms of the species. Some of these new forms stabilized as separate species. They were incapable, then, of reproducing with other descendants of the original lineage. This explains the abundance of diverse species in this environment.

When rainy periods followed dry periods, the forest cover would reestablish itself. The new species that had originated in isolation would encounter each other. Some crossbred. Others entered into competition, and the weakest died out. Some survived and stabilized in very specialized ecological niches. The process of differentiation, or developing many new species from a single species, was most intense when the phases of the rainforest's expansion and contraction due to climatic fluctuations were most numerous. The process of species differentiation can take ten thousand years for small animals and somewhat longer for larger ones. The succession of generations takes longer in larger animals because their life span is longer.

Climatic variation has been the principal reason for the proliferation of species in the Amazon. The development of the Andes, which greatly modified natural environments, also contributed. Animals and plants have survived and flourished as a result of the continuous existence of large, localized habitats and the general stability of the region.

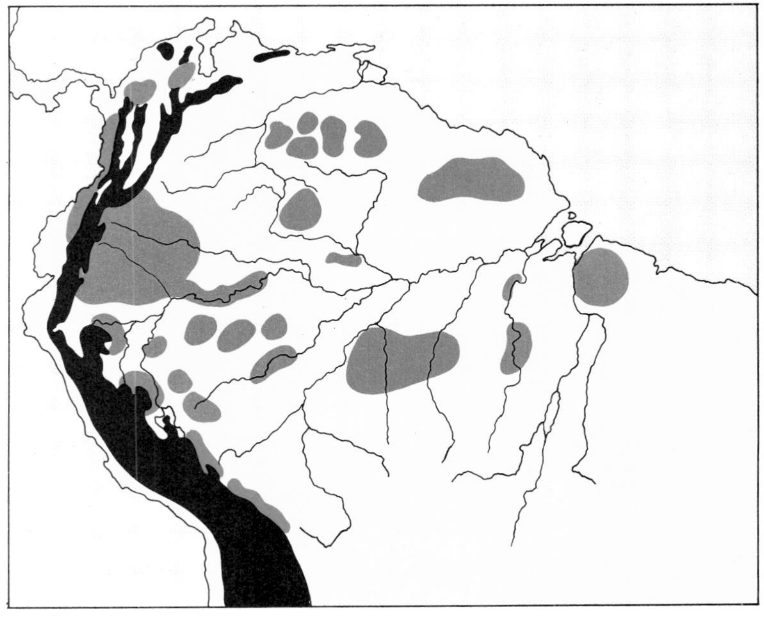

During the most recent geological eras, the great Amazon forest underwent a series of expansions and retractions. These were caused by the climatic fluctuations of the Quaternary period and to the glaciations that affected the northern hemisphere. During the retractions, large green "islands" survived to become places of shelter and species differentiation. The resulting species then mingled together, and, in many cases, lived together in different ecological niches. The extraordinary variety of different species, which is typical of the Amazon, derives from this differentiation process. The map shows the probable sites of the sheltering islands *(in red)* and the Andes mountain chain *(in black)*.

THE "FRESHWATER OCEAN"

Opposite page: The Guapore River floods the new state of Rondonia. Farmers' houses are half-submerged in the water. The Guapore River is a tributary of the Amazon. It first flows into the Mamore River, which, in turn, enters the Madeira River. The Madeira is one of the most important tributaries of the Amazon.

The Amazon River is 4,000 miles (6,437 km) long. Only the Nile River is longer, by about 150 miles (240 km). However, length is the only record the Amazon does not hold. Its water collecting basin covers 2,722,000 sq. miles (7,050,000 sq. km). Of this, 1,930,500 sq. miles (5,000,000 sq. km) are covered by impenetrable forests. The network of its tributaries is extremely complex. It collects water coming from the Andes as well as from other mountains and plateaus. No fewer than eleven hundred tributaries flow into the Amazon. Some of these rank among the largest rivers in the world. Seventeen of these tributaries are longer than the Rhine River, in western Europe. The volume of water carried by the Amazon River is colossal. It is calculated at 169 billion gallons (640 billion liters) per hour. Its rate of flow is forty-five times that of the Zaire River and ten times higher than that of the Mississippi River. The Thames River, in England, does not carry in a year the volume of water that the Amazon carries in a day. One-fifth of all the water that flows upon the surface of the earth passes through its mouth.

This enormous mass of fresh water forms a lake of approximately 62 sq. miles (160 sq. km) off the Atlantic coast. One can imagine the surprise and joy felt by the first navigators who sailed this "freshwater ocean." The first European explorer of the river was the Spaniard Francesco de Orellana, companion of Francisco Pizzaro, the "conquistador" of Peru. In 1541, De Orellana sailed down the Amazon for more than 3,700 miles (6,000 km). It was an incredible accomplishment for his time. On the way, he found himself face to face with various Indian tribes and, in particular, with bands of women who fought as fiercely as the men. For this reason, he named the river and its vast surrounding basin Amazonia in remembrance of the legendary warriors of classical mythology.

A Humble Source

It has long been known that the source of the Amazon River was located in the Peruvian Andes. Determining its exact location has been more difficult. Initially, it was believed to be in the towering Huayhuash chain. There, glaciers and rocky peaks rise to 21,000 feet (6,400 m), and high, inaccessible valleys are laced with lakes into which numerous torrents empty. The Amazon River was once thought to originate from one of these lakes, the Lauricocha.

Not many years ago, the French explorer Bertrand

The immense Amazon River mirrors a layer of clouds. The Amazon Basin is essentially flat. Streams cross it slowly, lazily, except in some areas, where rapids and cataracts form. It is remarkable that the phenomenon of high and low tides can be witnessed up to 620 miles (1000 km) from the river's mouth.

Flornoy ventured into these remote regions. He found, after scanning the shores of Lake Lauricocha, that it was fed by a tributary. That meant that the source of the Amazon River had to be located higher up. Following the water's course to a height of 1,657 feet (5,050 m), he discovered a glacial cirque, a deep, steep-walled basin shaped like a bowl. At the foot of this cirque there was a lake. Flornoy claims that the pebbles and the frozen snow along the shore "seemed to form a cradle beyond which there was nothing but ice and sheer rock." He had located the source.

The torrent becomes a swift river that descends the mountain along dizzying slopes. At first, it runs due north. It then turns eastward and maintains this course all the way to the sea. At first, the river is called the Marañón. In this initial stage, it takes on the waters of a very important tributary, the Ucayali River. The Ucayali is made up of two notable streams that also originate in the Andes, the Apurmac and the Urubamba. The Urubamba, in one of its meanderings through the mountains, loops around the rock spur upon which the ancient Incan village of Macchu Picchu is built. With the plentiful input of water from these primary tributaries, the Amazon River grows enormously. Heavy rain can increase its volume by sixfold.

The Plains of the Great Basin

The Marañón and its tributaries are fed by abundant rains from the Atlantic side of the Andes. The river runs for a short distance among majestic mountains and streambeds carved through deep canyons. The noise of the numerous rapids is often deafening.

A little farther on, the great river makes its entry onto the immense Amazonian plain. The steepness of its descent ends abruptly. From a point slightly above the western part of the basin, its slope is about one inch every four miles all the way to the river's mouth. Still, the waters continue to flow quickly, aided by the shape of the riverbed.

Before crossing the border into Brazil, the Amazon River is joined by several important tributaries. The first is the Napo, which originates in Ecuador. At the point where the river is called the Solimoles, it takes on the waters of the Putumayo, the Caqueta (so-named in Colombia, but called the Japura by Brazilians), the Jurua, and the Purus. A little farther on, deep in the heart of Amazonia, the great Negro River flows into the Amazon. On its banks, near the confluence (merging) of the two rivers, rises Manaus, the principal center and true capital of the Amazon region. The union of the two rivers is impressive. The water of the Amazon, which is still called the Solimoes at this point, is yellow. It is colored by the sediment swept along from the crumbly soils of the great plains. The sediment in the Negro River, however, is greenish black. This is because the river has crossed ancient rocky terrains that are very resistant to erosion. When flying over or navigating in the region where the two rivers converge, one can see numerous whirlpools and tall waves clearly marking their meeting place. Past this meet-

Near Marajo Island and other vast islands in the huge Amazon River estuary, a great many smaller islands form and disappear, depending on the high- and low-water periods. Here and there are floating islands made of logs and leaves that have been swept away from the river's shores. These large, unstable rafts flow with the current and eventually end up in the open sea. The river mouth, from which two-fifths of the flowing water of South America enters the ocean, is a world unto itself, immense and very complex.

ing point, the rivers flow on separately, side by side, for a long way. Fifty miles (80 km) downstream they finally begin to merge. It is here, at its confluence with the Negro River, that the Amazon River takes its name.

Now the great river makes its own way, free to course across the measureless plain. From the north, it receives the Trombetas. From the south come the tributaries of the Madeira, the Tapajos, and the Xingu.

Toward the Mouth

There remains only one obstacle for the river as it flows to the sea. The Andes are by now far behind, but ahead rise the remains of the Precambrian shields of Guyana and Brazil. At this point, the riverbed narrows, and the surrounding plain is reduced to a few miles on either side. It is here that the town of Obidos was founded to control the river traffic in 1697.

Past these narrow straits, the Amazon widens into a broad bed that, little by little, begins to resemble an inland sea. From a boat, at this point in the river, it is often impossible to see the shore. At times, the dark line of the impenetrable forest is only barely visible. This is the beginning of an immense estuary. It is broken up into many branches by islands whose dimensions change continually. The largest of these, Marajo, has an area of 18,530 sq. miles (48,000 sq. km). It is the largest river island in the world.

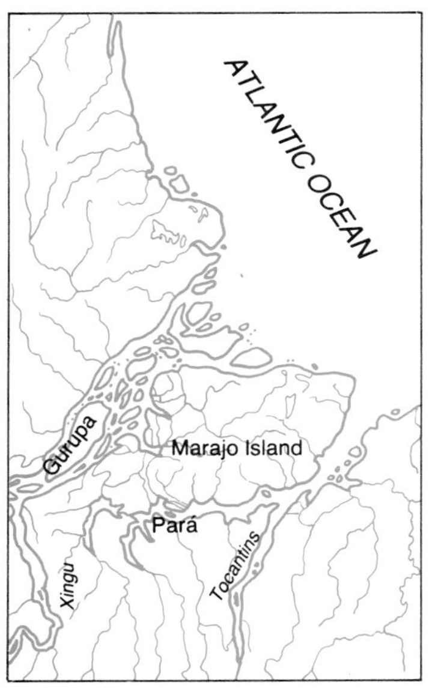

In Rhythm with the Seasons

Although the Amazon is characterized by a humid climate, only the northeastern part of the region is affected by high rainfall throughout the year. Elsewhere, there is a dry season with scattered and less abundant rains. This alternation of wet and dry seasons sets up a rhythm that determines the quantity of water carried by the Amazon and its tributaries. It affects the timing for periods of high water, which creates flooding, and low water.

This rhythm of the seasons in Amazonia is not always the same throughout the basin. In the south, the rains occur from September or October through April or May; in the east, from December through June; and in the north, from April through September. As a result, the volume of water transported varies greatly according to the location in the basin and the input of tributaries coming from the wettest areas. Toward the mouth, there is a maximum flow in May and a minimum in October and November. Floodwaters

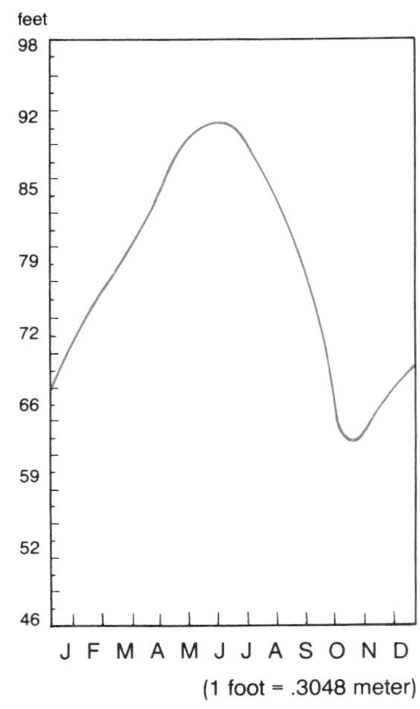

The variation in the volume of water carried by the Amazon River, dependent on rainfall draining from surrounding basins, is always considerable. A good example is the fluctuation observed on the Negro River, near Manaus, not far from this river's confluence with the Amazon River. There, the difference between maximum and minimum flow can vary as much as 33 feet (10 m) in depth. The consequent flooding of the lowlands and their forests turns them into *várzeas.*

can be impressive on the Solimoes where it can reach 66 feet (20 m) above its average level. High water tends to diminish toward the east. Even though the volume of water is extremely variable, water temperature is remarkably constant. For the entire year, the waters of the Amazon River remain close to 85°F (29°C).

In a territory as extensive and flat as Amazonia, river floods have enormous impact. For miles, the shores are overrun with extended lakes. Often, when navigating, it is impossible to know whether one is passing over a riverbed or a flood zone. An entire section of the basin, covering more than 19,300 square miles (50,000 sq. km), is affected by these rising and falling water levels.

The várzeas, so-called by the inhabitants of this region, host vegetation especially adapted to tolerate these fluctuations. The people have had to accommodate the continuous changes in the water level by establishing their homes and farmland on high terrain. Even there, they cannot be safe from severe floods.

Finally, the Amazon reaches the sea. Its lower course is periodically flooded by high Atlantic tides. A gigantic wave moves up the river as far as 620 miles (1,000 km). It is stopped only by the narrowing of the river that occurs between two ancient rocky shields.

Diverse Rivers and Streams

Of the rivers that cross Amazonia, many have quite different geomorphological features. The rivers of the upper part of the basin come down through the Andes, carving deep canyons and jagged valleys. As soon as they reach the plain, they seem to rest. The roar of their waters quiets, and they start meandering endlessly. Their intricate loops change position with each flooding. This leaves stretches of still water that will reconnect to the main stream with the next downpour.

In the central part of the basin, there is an abrupt change. For as yet undetermined reasons, the loops of the river and its tributaries, which are still fully loaded with water, become infrequent. One explanation involves the high speed of the current plus the heavy load of sediment carried by this section of the river. At this point, the surrounding plain is 12.5 to 63 miles (20 to 100 km) wide. It is enclosed between ancient river deposits dating back to the Tertiary period. These deposits mark the boundaries of the plain and form the so-called terra firma, or territory which is never flooded by the river. The stretch of land between the terra firma and the river is covered by more recent and very crumbly sediment. When the river flows over this ancient sediment, it carves into it and creates the "barreiras," as named by the Brazilians.

The rivers descending from the ancient crystalline mountains of Brazil and Guyana are much more stable. Their beds are carved in very hard rock. Often, they are marked at intervals with rapids that signal the shift from one geological layer to the next.

Sometimes large boulders divide the current into several courses. These can be navigated by canoe at different times of the year. From here, the rivers descend to the plain. As the sediment is deposited in elongated islands, deltas are formed. These environments are favorable to the development of aquatic life.

Rapids run the upper stretch of the Maroni River in the heart of the tropical forest. This river, 422 miles (680 km) long, originates in the Tumuc-Humac mountain chain on the border of Brazil and French Guyana.

Toward the mouth of the Amazon River, other interesting things occur. Fresh water of the river mingles with salt water from the sea. The sea plays the dominant role. This is exhibited by the phenomenon of the "pororoca." These are waves several yards high caused by the incoming tide. They are the terror of passengers in small boats. Floodwaters leave very little dry land. When they recede, they leave behind lakes and lagoons.

Interestingly, the color of the water varies in accordance with the river and the lands it crosses. There are rivers of white or ochre water called "rios de agua branca," that are murky and heavy with silt. Others have clear water of an olive green color. Still others have black, brown, or olive brown waters called "rios de agua preta." The latter are very acidic and carry sand.

When two rivers converge, their currents do not merge

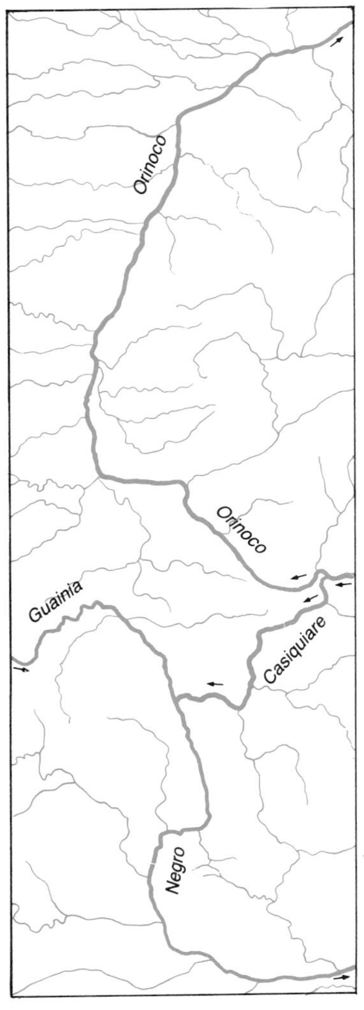

The Casiquiare is a natural canal, unique in the world. Charles-Marie de la Condamine heard of its existence from the Indians but failed to locate it. Its "discovery" is attributed to Alexander von Humboldt and A.J. Alexandre Bonpland. Today, the Casiquiare, navigable for 140 miles (225 km), is traveled by ships of low tonnage.

together instantly. This is the case of the two giants, the Solimoes and Negro rivers, that form the Amazon River.

From the Orinoco to the Amazon

North of Amazonia extends the basin of the Orinoco, another giant South American river. It is 1,600 miles (2,575 km) long. The river originates in the Serra Parima Mountains, collects the greater part of its water from Venezuela, and courses into the Atlantic Ocean after tracing a wide curve.

The rather indefinite line that divides the Amazon basin from that of the Orinoco lies within a wide, eroded plateau. There appear to be no true springs there. There are, however, flooded surfaces that are thickly covered with palms. Here, the water seems to hesitate before deciding whether to flow into one basin or the other.

There is another peculiar connection between the two basins. A little beyond the city of Esmeralda, Venezuela, where the Orinoco has already become a large river, a stream called the Casiquiare diverges from it and heads south. It adds its waters to those of the Amazon River basin, flowing first into the Guaina River, a tributary of the Negro River.

A Network of Navigable Rivers

For a long time, the only means of penetrating the Amazon were via the myriad streams, both large and small, that flow across it. Even today, in spite of the construction of trans-Amazonian roadways, the importance of the waterways for commerce and exploration remains fundamental.

Today, the visitor still encounters all types of ships and convoys of barges, fighting upstream against the currents with loads of consumer goods needed by inhabitants of the region. They will return later, full of lumber, farm produce, and other riches from the forests. A flotilla of small boats ventures on the smaller rivers. The safest and most picturesque means of getting from one place to another, either for pleasure or necessity, remains the "*pirogue*" (an Indian craft made of logs or reeds).

For many animal species of the forests, the larger Amazonian rivers have been impenetrable barriers. This may not be true for the amphibians, but it is for the birds. Because their survival is linked to the forest foliage or to the thick vegetation of the underbrush, it is difficult for them to venture out on the waters, where their lives are endangered.

The great rivers of the Amazon have formed effective natural barriers for many animals. This has prolonged the impact of the wide climatic fluctuations of the Pleistocene upon the process of species differentiation. Even the birds have been affected, as is shown by the distribution of trumpeters of the genus *Psophia*. Distribution of species and subspecies of this genus is clearly influenced by important rivers. Differentiation, often limited to the level of subspecies, may extend to the formation of entirely new species. On the map, the mountainous massifs of the Andes are indicated in black.

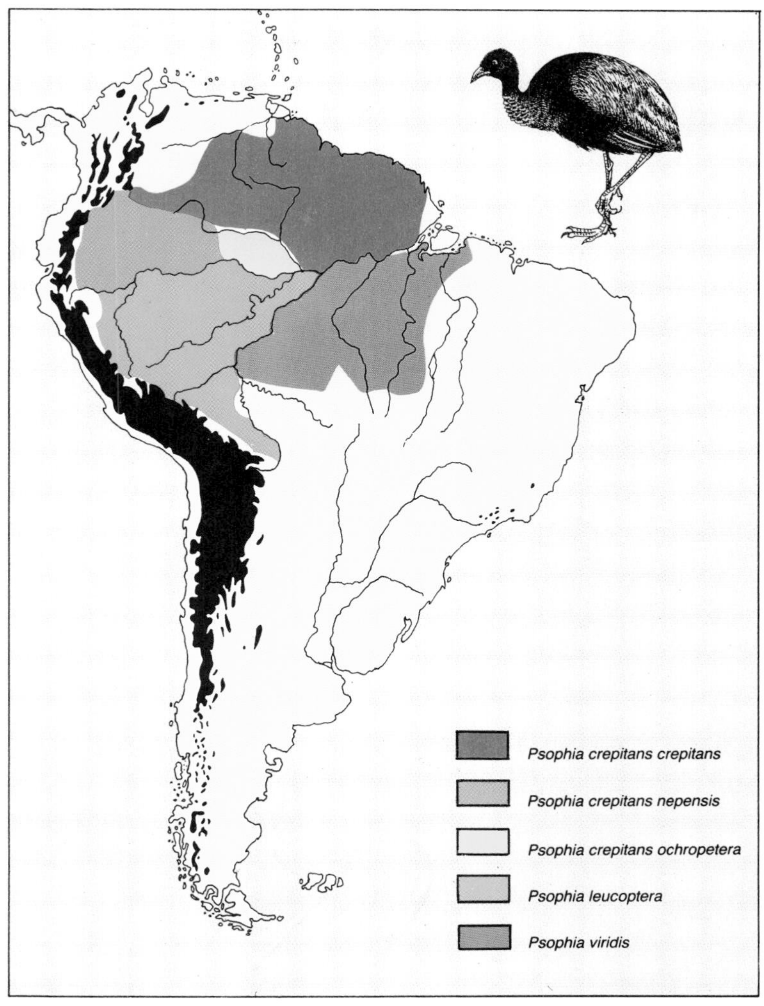

Other animals, such as monkeys, share similar limitations.

Thus, over the course of time, a great mosaic of biological islands has been created. Each island may contain a particular species that is replaced by another distinct species at an adjacent waterway. By creating these impassable boundaries for many animals, the great rivers of Amazonia have continued the fragmentation of the forest that began during the drier periods of its ancient history.

AQUATIC PLANTS AND ANIMALS

Along with the sun, water controls the richness of the Amazon, whether one speaks of large rivers or of small pools of still water covered with vegetation. One part of the forest, the várzeas, is periodically affected by river floods. Sometimes it is dry land, and sometimes it is an aquatic area. Other zones, called "igapos," are always aquatic.

Among plants, flowering plants undoubtedly play the most important role. These are adapted to every type of environment. They are found both in the periodically flooded forests and on the alluvial (material deposited by running water) shores. At certain times, these shores are covered with grasses of various types such as those of the genera *Paspalum*, and *Echinochloa*, as well as wild rice. The life cycles of these grasses are strictly tied to the water cycles. There are also palms, such as *Maurizia flexuosa.*

Plants Adapted to Aquatic Life

Many plants cannot live outside the water. This is the case with members of the Aracaea family. Members of this family, such as the moucou-moucou of Guyana, form enormous clumps along the rivers that stabilize the mud on the banks.

Even the open water is often clogged with algae and more complex plants. Among these is the water hyacinth, whose leaves are equipped with flotation devices. Its roots, which absorb necessary nutrients from the water, are anchored in the bottom silt. Its flowers are a beautiful blue-mauve color. Because of its beauty, this plant has been exported to various tropical areas as an ornamental species.

The waters of the Amazon are also inhabited by various water lilies. Among these are found the largest species of the family, Victoria regia. Its floating leaves reach up to 6.5 feet (2 m) in diameter. Their edges are folded upward so that they resemble gigantic pie tins. The veins of the leaf and its overall structure are so sturdy that it can easily support the weight of a child. These giant water lilies cover wide surfaces of rivers and pools. Like all members of their family, these plants have a very peculiar reproductive system. Their short-lived flowers open only for a few hours and are quickly fertilized before being retracted into the water. The ripe seed eventually surfaces by the action of a flotation device and is carried by the water for a time before falling back to the bottom. There, it will sink into the silt and germinate, starting a new plant. A very common and typical plant in still waters is the fern, *Salvinia natans*. This spe-

Opposite page: Shown is a stretch of water hyacinths form a thick mat in the Amazon forest. In some of the areas where this species was introduced by humans, it has caused serious environmental problems. These problems show the risks of dispersing living species far from their places of origin, where their growth is controlled by natural factors.

Victoria regia, equipped with huge leaves that can be up to 6 feet (2 m) wide, is a giant water lily widely spread throughout still or slow running water in the Amazon Basin. This plant is so sturdy that it can support the weight of a child. Thus, it makes a useful landing site for the numerous aquatic animals of the region.

cies, which multiplies extremely quickly, forms green carpets that can completely cover the water surface.

A unique group of plants belonging to the family Podostemonaceae dwells in the turbulent waters and upon the rapids. At first sight, these plants resemble mosses or some algae, but they are true flowering plants. They are extremely simple and have effectively adapted to survive in a hostile environment such as that of rapids and waterfalls.

The Atlantic side of the Amazon forest is the realm of the mangroves. They inhabit the riverbanks wherever the water is sufficiently brackish, or salty. Often, a stretch of savanna will sneak in between the forests and the mangrove swamps. The most common genera are *Rhizophora* and *Avicennia*. The first is characterized by branching supports that buttress its trunk. The latter has roots that rise vertically from the swampy terrain and sometimes possess respiratory functions, called pneumatophores.

Animals of the River

Due to the variety of bodies of water in the Amazon, there are a great number of animal species that thrive there.

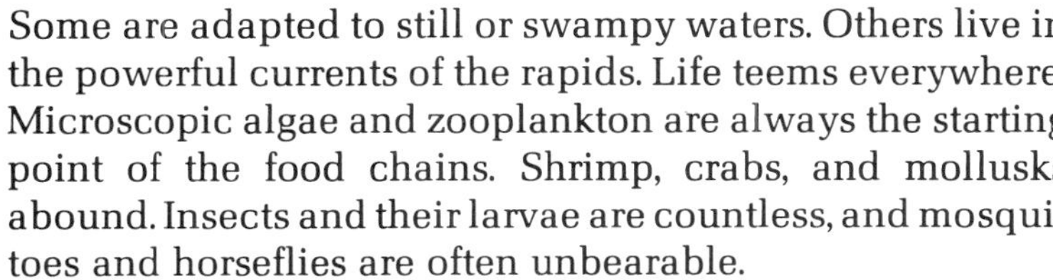

Some are adapted to still or swampy waters. Others live in the powerful currents of the rapids. Life teems everywhere. Microscopic algae and zooplankton are always the starting point of the food chains. Shrimp, crabs, and mollusks abound. Insects and their larvae are countless, and mosquitoes and horseflies are often unbearable.

This multitude of life-forms sometimes includes animals that do not ordinarily inhabit such areas. Sharks, spiny skates, sole, herring, anchovies, manatees, and dolphins are all present in the Amazon.

For reasons of survival, many animals not truly aquatic are tied to the water. These include tapirs, peccaries, jaguars, and the great anteaters. The class of reptiles is well represented by snakes, caimans, and turtles.

A Myriad of Fish

Amazonia's size and the diversity of its aquatic environments provide the great number of ecological niches that favor a multitude of fish. All of the families are represented except for the Cyprinidae, which includes carp. The number of known species is around twelve hundred, but new ones are being identified. When the list is complete, the

Lower left: Plants belonging to the family Podostemonadeae cling to the rocks in white water with their suckerlike roots. Tiny plants often develop from such roots.

Lower right: *Mourera fluviatilis* is a species of the family Podostemonadeae. The flowers of this peculiar dweller of the rapids have a very short life cycle. During low-water periods, when most of the plant is exposed to the air, flowers blossom. The fertilization of flowers and the ripening of seeds happens very quickly. Following this, the mother plants dry out. The new seedlings will soon attach to the rocks, starting another generation of plants that have no rivals in the white water environment.

Piranhas show their characteristic sharp teeth in an Amazonian lagoon. During flooding, these highly feared little animals are able to clear the flooded regions of dead animals. They eat fish and other weak or wounded animals that could spread disease. They leave no leftovers.

total number will probably be near two thousand. In comparison, the number of known species in the Zaire River, formerly the Congo River, in Central Africa is 850. Some species are gargantuan in size. The most famous is the pirarucu, called the "paiche" in Peru and the "arapaima" in Guyana. This fish can reach 10 feet (3 m) in length and 220 pounds (100 kilograms) in weight. Its powerful body is green in the front and red toward the back. It is highly prized by fishers for its meat.

Catfish are represented in considerable numbers in Amazonia. Some, like *Brachyplatystoma filamentosum* and related species, occasionally reach gigantic dimensions. Their name is due to the elongations of their lips, which resemble whiskers.

The most numerous family is the Characidae. It includes almost half the fish that live in Amazonia, both in terms of species and number. These fish occupy the most diverse ecological niches. In some cases, they have lost their teeth and feed upon microscopic organisms by filtering silt from the riverbed. Many populate still waters covered with vegetation. Some, highly sought after as aquarium fish, compete with birds of the forest in colorations.

A catfish swims the Amazon waters. Some fish, belonging to the same group, have an armor of bony plates covering their body. This armor protects them against the sharp rocks of the rapids, where they venture to feed on aquatic plants. Other species, a few inches long, are carnivores. These are parasites that spend all of their lives clinging to the gills of larger fish.

The Serrasalmidae include fish like the pacu, or dollar fish, that feed on leaves and fruit as well as ferocious carnivores like the famous piranhas (*Serrasalmus* and similar genera). Piranhas, about 1 foot (30 cm) in length, have sturdy jaws and extremely sharp teeth that can cut through flesh like a scalpel.

One rather curious fish is the four-eyed fish. It is called this because its eyes are divided into separate sections containing the cornea and retina. Swimming near the water's surface, it surveys the environment above the water with the upper parts of its eyes. The lower parts see all that occurs in the water's depths. This strange fish also demonstrates a curious means of reproduction. It is viviparous. This means the female keeps the eggs in her body until after they hatch and the young are fully developed.

The more peaceful streams are inhabited by another unique fish, the electric eel. It is similar in shape to the common eel. The electric eel can attain lengths of up to 6.6 feet (2 m). This fish can deliver shocks of around 350 volts. The muscles in the forward part of its body form plates aligned like the elements of an electric battery.

This fish belongs to the genus *Anableps*. Because of the fish's strange looking eyes, it is called a four-eyed fish.

Another unusual fish has a dual respiratory system. Like its African relatives, *Lepidosiren paradoxa*, of the order Dipnoi, has a kind of lung in addition to gills for respiration. This lung, similar to that of amphibians, allows the intake of oxygen from the air. When drought periods cause the water to recede, this fish burrows in the mud, reduces its respiratory rate, and begins to use its lung like a land animal.

Finally, it is important to emphasize the relative scarcity of phytoplankton and zooplankton (microscopic free-floating algae and animals, respectively) in the Amazonian waters. Thus, during flooding, many fish head toward the várzeas and the inundated parts of the forest in search of

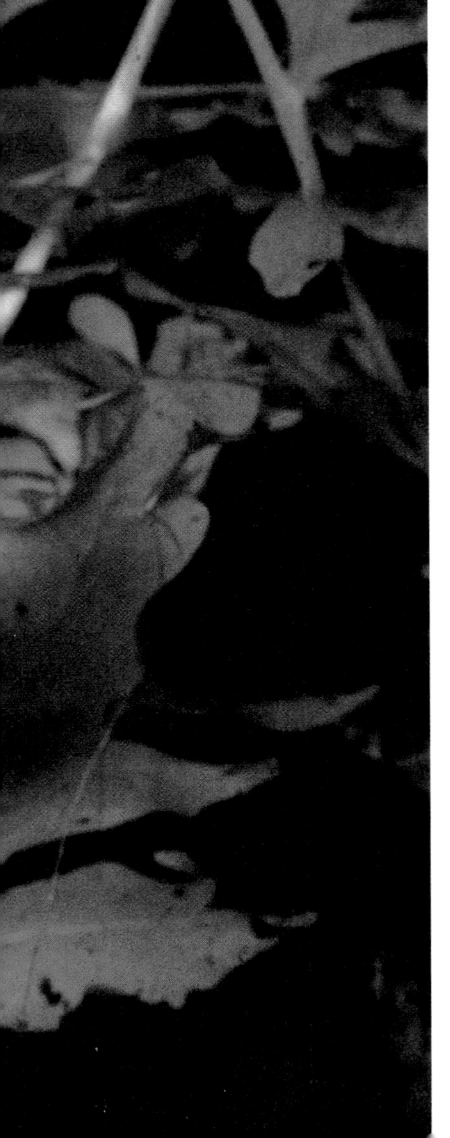

food. Like their ecological couterparts in Eurasia, for example those of the Mekong River, these fish swim across the flooded plains, feeding on fruit and other plant matter.

Toads and Frogs

Amazonian amphibians have interested researchers very little, certainly much less than other animal species. In spite of the fact that their habits are often engaging and their biological importance is undeniable, scientists have begun studying them only lately. Before recent studies, only one inventory had been taken of the toads and frogs. It was in Guyana. The list included seventy species, a very low number considering that the number living in the Amazon is at least double that. Spread throughout the most diverse environments, the anurans (tailless amphibians) are found most easily after dusk. Then, their calls can be heard. As with birds, each species has a characteristic sound that enables it to recognize other individuals of its own species. This prevents crossbreeding. A nocturnal visit to a small stream can be a fascinating experience. Dozens of little shimmering points move about in the beam of the flashlight. These are mostly toads that gather on smooth stones to enjoy the humidity. Their numbers are astounding.

Dependent upon the water for their reproduction, toads and frogs have adapted to this dependency in diverse ways. Some deposit their eggs directly in the water where they become attached to plants. Others secrete a foamy white mass, similar to whipped egg whites, around their eggs. This maintains the humidity and oxygen level necessary for development. The rather suspect appearance of this mass is also a good defense against predators. Still others behave in even more complex ways.

Some amphibians stay close to their litters, carrying them around on their backs. In some cases, the eggs are laid within depressions in the skin. In others, the skin of the back folds like a kangaroo's pouch, and the eggs are incubated there until they hatch. The tadpoles are then gently set in the water. In other, even more specialized species, the entire development of the frog is completed in the pouch. Small, fully formed frogs emerge from it. Among the Indians, this phenomenon gave birth to the myth that the offspring of such amphibians came from their backs and not by the usual means!

Rafting along a river, travelers cannot help but lift their eyes toward the lush foliage of the forest. Even the trees, laden with humidity and rich in food resources, are hosts to some amphibians. For example, there are the Dendrobatidae. Some of these are still dependent on an aquatic environment. Others, more adapted to trees, deposit their eggs in water that collects on the branches. Within these small pools, epiphytic plants called "bromeliads" grow. Epiphytic plants are those that grow nonparasitically upon other plants and obtain nutrients from the surrounding water and air. These "suspended reservoirs" are themselves small ecosystems teeming with larvae, insects, and tadpoles.

Tree frogs abound in the trees. Represented in Europe by only one species *(Hyla arborea)*, they are widely and variously represented in Amazonia. There are minute species that live among the bushes. Others, 6 inches (15 cm) long, inhabit the tree foliage. Some have mimetic coloration that resembles leaves and cork. These species baffle their predators by changing even their shape, thanks to fringes of skin. On the other hand, some tree frogs are extravagantly colored.

Tree frogs have adapted extraordinarily well to life above ground. Large webbed feet and toes that double as suction cups assure a solid grip on leaves and branches. The elongation of the toes also facilitates the firm grip. In certain species, the thumb has become opposable to the other digits. This allows the foot to grasp twigs easily.

In addition to those species that deposit their eggs in pools among tree branches, some roll them up in cones of

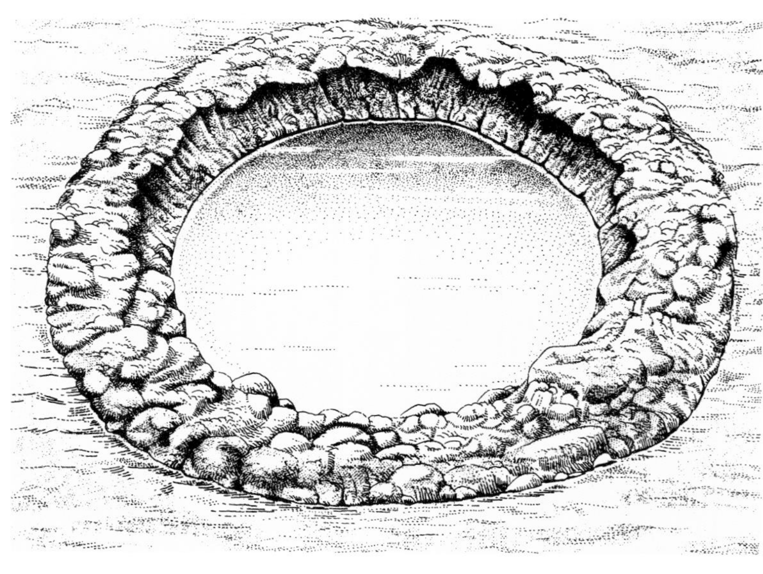

Some tree frogs, for example *Hyla boans*, build a nest—or more appropriately, a "pool"—by digging a small hole in the sand. It is 12 to 20 inches (30 to 50 cm) in diameter and 3 to 4 inches (7 to 10 cm) deep, protected by a wall about 2.5 inches (6 cm) tall. After the male has completed this work, it settles in the center and begins to call the female. The eggs hatch within a few days. The tadpoles, kept safely away from predators, also benefit from the warmer water, which aids in their development. The leaves that fall into the pool are their food supply until they develop into young frogs. They then continue their growth under the dead leaves or in the pools of stagnant water nearby.

Sometimes called "painted frogs," many Dendrobatidae have particularly lively coloration that warns predators. Their skin contains highly toxic substances linked to their pigments. The Indians used these in the preparation of poisons for hunting, often mixing them with curare (a poison that has a paralytic effect). The toxic extract from the skin of *Phyllobates aurotaenia*, for example, is 5,000 times more powerful than cyanide and 250 times more powerful than curare. Some people have died merely by handling this animal. In the photograph, a *Dendrobates granuliferus* carries a tadpole on its back.

curled leaves and suspend them above the water. After hatching, the tadpoles fall into the water. They will complete their development there until they are ready to climb the trees. Still other tree frogs are completely independent of the water. They bear eggs upon their backs, either openly or enclosed in a pocket. This is the case with the marsupial tree frog.

Birds

Because of the variety of environments and the abundance of food, many diverse species of birds are found in wetlands. The sandy banks are inhabited by ducks. One group includes tree ducks. Within this group, the fulvous whistling duck gathers in dense flocks during certain periods of the year. Many of the Amazon ducks are similar in appearance to those found in Europe. The Brazilian teal has

fulvous whistling duck

Brazilian duck

muscovy duck

gray-breasted crake

azure galinule

dark plumage. The male is typically white with a greenish blue metallic sheen. A fine swimmer, this teal always keeps close to the water and nests on the ground. It is often found perched upon tree branches. The mute duck is more of a tree dweller. Its plumage is black, speckled with iridescent green and blue dots. The male is larger than the female. It weighs about 11 pounds (5 kg); the female weighs about half of that. The bill of the male is crowned with a bright red fleshy protuberance. This species feeds on grasses on the ground and spends the night perched on tree branches. It builds its nest inside the largest holes in the trees. It is easily domesticated and is often raised by the Indians.

A quick reference to the rails is appropriate (*Laterallus, Aramides*, and their related genera, *Gallinula, Porphyrula*, etc.). These birds are extremely shy and spend most of their lives hidden in the thickest vegetation. They venture out only at night.

Finfoots deserve special mention. Though these birds have webbed feet like the coots, they are only distantly related. The finfoots are primitive birds that like to perch on branches and are swift swimmers. Among them is found *Heliornis fulica*. Other members of this group inhabit tropical zones in Africa and Asia.

An especially interesting finfoot is the sun bittern. This is an elegant bird approximately 20 inches (50 cm) in length, with a graceful and slender shape. The sun bittern may be found either near the water or in the midst of the most humid forests. It feeds upon insects, crustaceans, and small fish that it skewers with its harpoonlike beak. It lives in the shelter of the forest canopy but performs its mating ritual in full daylight. It fans out its wide wings and tail feathers that are delicately shaded brown, black, gray, and white. The female, no less colorful than the male, deposits her eggs in a nest constructed in the trees. This nest may be 40 feet (12 m) above the ground.

Among the wading birds abundant in Amazonia, there are the jacanas. In particular, there is the American jacana that can run on the water lilies thanks to its large feet and extremely elongated claws. The jabiru, a stork, is the largest American member of the Ciconidae family, and it is also represented in the Amazon Basin. There is one species of ibis, the American wood ibis.

Members of the family Ardeidae are frequently encountered. One of these, the cattle egret, came to the New World from Africa only a few decades ago. In addition,

herons, night herons, and little bitterns are found.

The roseate spoonbill and the scarlet ibis are birds of particularly splendid coloration. The latter is found along the Atlantic coast, and its brilliant color enlivens lagoons and leafy canopies of the mangrove swamps. Its marvelous plumes, used in the fabrication of artificial flowers, have made it the object of heedless hunting. This has substantially reduced its numbers.

The spoonbill *Cochieanus cochieanus*, is 20 inches (50 cm) tall. It is easily recognized by its huge spoon-shaped beak, which is 2 inches (5 cm) wide and 3 inches (7.5 cm) long. It lives primarily on the mangrove-covered coast, but it may also be found along rivers. Its principal foods include worms, crustaceans, and fish. Its highly specialized beak probably also helps in sifting through bottom silt in search of other prey.

The waters of Amazonia are rich in mollusks of every type. Many birds, including some of those already described, include mollusks in their diets. Some have attained a high level of specialization in competing for these invertebrates. The best example is the limpkin *Aramus guarauna*, which is distantly related to the rails. Two feet tall (60 cm), this bird moves freely on even the most unstable mud. Thanks to its long claws, it does not sink down into the soft earth. Its diet consists almost exclusively of mollusks that it extracts from the bottom with great skill. It uses its sturdy beak to break shells. Its characteristically mournful song, which it emits after dusk and throughout the night, has earned it the nickname of "crying bird."

Another bird that feeds primarily on mollusks is *Rostrhamus hamatus*. This is a bird of prey with blackish plumage and a contrasting reddish growth at the base of its beak. It feeds mainly upon gastropods (mollusks with a spiral shell, such as the snail). After seizing a shell, it grasps it in its claws and waits for the animal to emerge. Then it pierces it with its beak, which ends in a kind of hook, and removes it from the shell.

The hoatzin is one of the most peculiar species of birds in the world. This bird is the size of a pheasant and has multicolored plumage, predominantly blue and white. On its head, it has an erect crest. For a long time it was thought to be related to the cuckoo, whose shape it resembles. More recent studies, however, tend to suggest that it belongs to the Galliformes, a group that includes hens and turkeys. Still, this species is very hard to identify. It lives along riverbanks,

One hoatzin is in flight; another perches in a Peruvian forest (Manu National Park). These birds resemble the extinct archaeopteryx, a primitive bird with reptilian characteristics. Like the archaeopteryx, the young hoatzin has a wing equipped with claws that prove very useful in climbing.

especially among the moucou-moucou. It feeds on their leaves and young shoots. Its digestion is aided by a huge crop which is a modification of the throat by which food is first ground before entering the stomach. This crop forms a sack divided into two sections and sustained by strong muscles. The organ is so large that it constitutes one-third of the bird's body. It has caused the displacement of the breastbone and the reduction of the carina and flight muscles. For this reason, the hoatzin's flying ability is not good.

These features would be enough to attract the attention of scientists, but they are not all that is peculiar about the hoatzin. It builds a coarse nest on tree branches that lean out over the water. Newborn birds are able to get out of the nest by using their legs and, also, the hooks that grow from the tips of their wings. At this stage, and for some weeks, they are true quadrupeds (four-legged animals). They resemble reptiles more than birds. If they fall into the water, they can

swim ashore and climb up to their nest. This bird combines markedly primitive features with highly developed adaptations. The hoatzin provides proof that the Amazon forest is an environment that has permitted the preservation of primitive animals together with the evolution of highly differentiated species, each adapted to specific ecological conditions.

Mammals

Many mammals have adapted to a life-style that could be termed amphibious. They are at ease both on the ground and in the water, where they catch their food. The largest rodent in the world lives here. It is the capybara, which can grow to be 3 feet (1 m) long and weigh 110 pounds (50 kg). It somewhat resembles a hog, but its rounded shaped and the form of its head are reminiscent of a guinea pig. Its skin is visible through its sparse fur. The capybara lives on the riverbanks in groups of about thirty. It feeds exclusively on aquatic plants, grasses, and water hyacinths, as well as some legumes. Its usual predator on the ground is the jaguar. In the water, it falls victim to the caiman (a South American crocodile) and the anaconda. Females deliver four to eight babies during the rainy season. Some Amazonian countries, Venezuela in particular, have tried to raise this rodent in semicaptivity. It is an exceptional meat producer. That means that it very efficiently transforms vegetable matter into animal proteins.

Another aquatic mammal is the otter. This carnivore is very well represented throughout Amazonia. It is possible to encounter more than one species related to the European otter. There is *Lutra enudris*, of modest size, and the giant otter that grows to about 6 feet (1.8 m) and can weigh 70 pounds (32 kg). This splendid animal dwells mainly along small, quiet streams, called "igarapaas" by the Brazilians. It lives in families of four to eight individuals. Like all otters it is very playful. It is known to use a great variety of calls. Its primary diet is fish, and it eats up to 20 percent of its weight daily. For this reason its hunting territory is necessarily very wide. The female gives birth to from one to six young, inside a burrow dug near the water.

The giant otter has beautiful fur, for which it has been hunted for many years. Between 1960 and 1967, over forty thousand pelts were officially exported from Brazil. Today, the animal is protected. It is found only in very remote areas. It is remarkably unafraid of humans and is one of the most

An adult capybara, followed by a group of young, swims in a river in the Amazon region. The capybara is the largest of all rodents and can attain a length of 3 feet (1 m) and a weight of 110 pounds (50 kg). From a practical point of view, the capybara represents an excellent source of protein. In some areas of the Amazon, it is raised in the wilds. This provides strong economic incentive for preservation of the forests.

interesting animals of the Amazon region.

The only marsupial of markedly amphibious habits lives here and is called the "yapok," or water opossum. It has brown-and-white-striped fur, grows up to 12 inches (30 cm) long, and has a tail up to 16 inches (40 cm) long. Like the otter, it lives by the water, digging a burrow in the thick of the vegetation. Like all other marsupials, the female has a marsupium, or abdominal pocket, where its young seek shelter after they are born. Its marsupium is waterproof, so

the young stay dry even during the water acrobatics performed by their mother.

Besides the amphibious mammals just described, there are others more restricted to an aquatic environment. These also breathe air through their lungs, but they cannot survive out of water. Most important is the manatee, which the Brazilians call "peisen boi." Today, this animal dwells in every corner of the tropical forest. Its spread is blocked only by the river rapids. It is related to a species that lives along

A pink dolphin is photographed in the aquarium at Manaus. This cetacean (whalelike mammal) of the family Platanistidae has given rise to a multitude of legends. The Indians maintain that it can stay outside the water, singing sweet melodies like the sirens of classical mythology. Moreover, some claim that it is capable of changing into a wondrous woman who wanders through the villages at night, trying to lure fishermen and take them to the bottom of the sea. Fables aside, it is quite extraordinary that a cetacean can be found swimming among the trees of a flooded forest looking for fish. The fish, in turn, are drawn by the fruit and other vegetable matter that they find in this flooded environment for most of the year.

the coasts of south America and to another that inhabits western Africa.

The manatee is quite large. It may be 13 feet (4 m) long and weigh up to about 882 pounds (400 km). It has front paws modified into fins, and the hind legs are joined to form a tail that is horizontally flattened. The head is huge, with a very large mouth and jaws equipped with crushing teeth. This mammal belongs to the order Sirenia. It has been placed by zoologists between the orders Hyracoidea (to which the shrew belongs) and Proboscidea (which includes the elephant) despite there being no apparent physical resemblance.

The manatee has a tranquil nature and sustains itself exclusively on aquatic plants. These include arums, legumes, water lilies, grasses, water hyacinths, and ferns. It

Unlike the dolphins, manatees are not cetaceans but rather sirenians. That is, they belong to a completely different group of aquatic mammals that, among other things, feeds only upon vegetable matter and not upon fish. The Amazonian manatee shown below consumes enormous quantities of aquatic plants. It is, therefore, used to contain plant growth in areas of Amazonia where this is necessary for human activity.

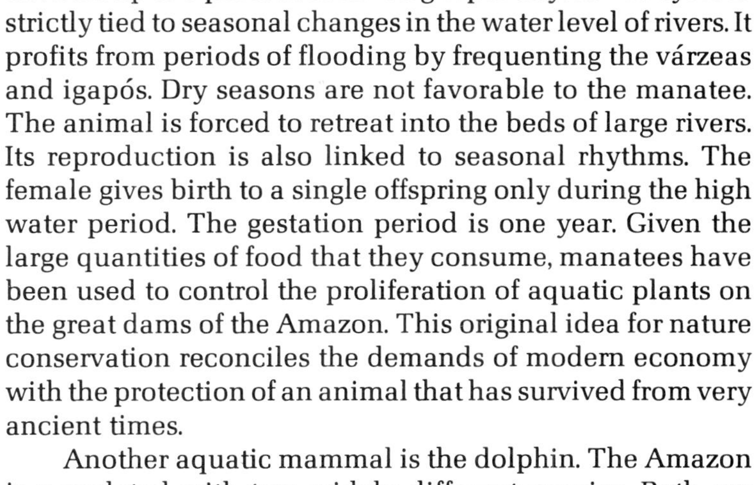

devours up to 8 percent of its weight per day. Its life cycle is strictly tied to seasonal changes in the water level of rivers. It profits from periods of flooding by frequenting the várzeas and igapós. Dry seasons are not favorable to the manatee. The animal is forced to retreat into the beds of large rivers. Its reproduction is also linked to seasonal rhythms. The female gives birth to a single offspring only during the high water period. The gestation period is one year. Given the large quantities of food that they consume, manatees have been used to control the proliferation of aquatic plants on the great dams of the Amazon. This original idea for nature conservation reconciles the demands of modern economy with the protection of an animal that has survived from very ancient times.

Another aquatic mammal is the dolphin. The Amazon is populated with two widely different species. Both are carnivorous. The first is the river dolphin, *Sotalia fluviatalis*. It is closely related to the marine species and does not exceed 5 feet (1.5 m) in length and 117 pounds (53 kg) in weight. It is easily recognized by its gray color and its relatively short snout. It is seen in small groups, often leaping above the water to play or to surprise small fish. The river dolphin feeds mainly on deep water fish that live in large schools. Like all dolphins, it uses a well-perfected hearing organ that allows for the rapid location of prey, even in turbulent waters. The second species is the pink dolphin, *Inia geoffrensis*.

Considered more primitive and at the same time, characteristic of fresh waters, the pink dolphin belongs to the order Cetacea, which includes all dolphins and whales. Its closest relatives are found in the Ganges River in India.

Its size, greater than the river dolphin's, can reach 8.5 feet (2.6 m) in length and 350 pounds (160 kg) in weight. The gray young acquire a pink color in adulthood, which is uncommon among dolphins. Its snout is longer than those of related species, and its neck is more mobile. It lives alone, feeding upon bottom fish. During periods of high water, it visits the flooded várzeas to pursue fish that come there to feed. The two Amazonian species of dolphins do not compete with each other. They feed on different species of fish, and they do not frequent the same habitats.

REPTILES

Reptiles are well represented in the Amazon by extremely diverse groups. There are turtles, caimans, lizards, and snakes. Some are aquatic; others are land or tree dwellers. Still others shift easily from one environment to the other. They play a very important role in the community, both as predators and as prey.

Aquatic Turtles

The most spectacular and best-known Amazonian turtles are those of the genus *Podocnemis*. Of these, the most widely distributed is the arrau turtle, *Podocnemis expansa*. It is considered very primitive because fossil remains have been found dating back to the Cretaceous period more than one hundred million years ago. This makes *Podocnemis expansa* a splendid example of an animal remarkably loyal to its original geographic range.

Growing to lengths of up to 32 inches (80 cm), *Podocnemis expansa* feeds on aquatic plants and fruit. During the mating season, these gregarious animals group together to deposit their eggs. It is sometimes possible to count thousands of individuals (up to eight thousand on some large sandbars). They clog the beds of large rivers, while the sound of their clacking carapaces, or shells, can be heard at a great distance. Their reproduction is linked to the rhythm of the seasons. The female goes in search of sunny sites that are necessary for the maturation of her eggs. These are deposited in burrows excavated in the sand, usually more than 3 feet (1 m) deep. The eggs are spherical and covered with a shell similar to parchment. An average of ninety eggs are deposited, but the number may vary between forty-eight and 132. After forty-eight days, heated by the sun and held at the proper level of humidity by the rains, the eggs hatch. The young move swiftly toward the water. They are 2 inches (5 cm) long and weigh about half an ounce (20 grams) at birth. It will take them from five to seven years to achieve full adult size.

In the Amazonian jungles there are also carnivorous turtles. These are gifted with great mobility and with long necks that enable them to capture mollusks, insects, and fish. This diet is supplemented with some vertebrates. The most representative of these is the mata-mata. It has a carapace about 20 inches (50 cm) long. Its neck is equipped with a sort of funnel that enables it to breathe under water. It feeds on crustaceans, tadpoles, and small fish, which it swallows whole.

Opposite page: The dwarf-caiman is one of the smallest and shyest of the armored reptiles in Amazonia. Unlike the huge and dangerous jacar, which attains lengths of 16 to 20 feet (5 to 6 m), this species rarely exceeds 3 feet (1 m) in length. It feeds mainly upon small aquatic animals. All of the caimans, not excluding smaller jacares, can fall prey to the jaguar, which seems to have a particular liking for them.

The common iguana rests in the midst of Amazonian vegetation. In the South American tropical forests, the lizards are represented by numerous families. One of the most versatile and rich in species is that of the Iguanidae. The species depicted here is one of the most widespread. It is a source of food for all of the human populations that inhabit the Amazon Basin.

Caimans

The crocodiles are represented by various species that at one time were quite numerous. That was before people began to hunt them for their skins and for the oil that can be extracted from their bodies. The black caiman, known in Brazil as the jacaré-acu is the largest at 20 feet (6 m) long. It frequents the still waters, várzeas, and igapós. The adults feed on large fish, aquatic turtles, and birds. They will even attack capybara, deer, and cattle domesticated by farmers when they come to drink from the river. The young catch smaller prey, in proportion to their size, such as small fish,

insects, crustaceans, and mollusks. Black caimans are gregarious animals that gather in groups on sandy riverbanks. During the reproductive period when the water level is low, females build nests on masses of leaves. They are usually 60 inches by 30 inches (150 cm by 75 cm). They lay thirty to sixty eggs and watch over them until they hatch. This takes place about five to six weeks later.

Another very common species is the spectacled caiman, so-called because of the wide bony protuberance that connects its eye sockets. This animal is 8 feet (2.5 m) long and thrives in various habitats. It favors still waters and lagoons. It lives in groups and feeds on invertebrates and medium-sized fish and mammals.

Unlike other caiman species, the dwarf-caiman and related species live in rivers with turbulent waters. Thanks to their rough skin, they can tolerate bumping their bodies on the rocks of the rapids. This caiman is about 5 feet (1.6 m) long. It is very shy and is not often seen basking in the sun like other caimans. A carnivore, it preys on a variety of animals. These include crustaceans, fish, birds, and mammals that it seizes on the riverbanks.

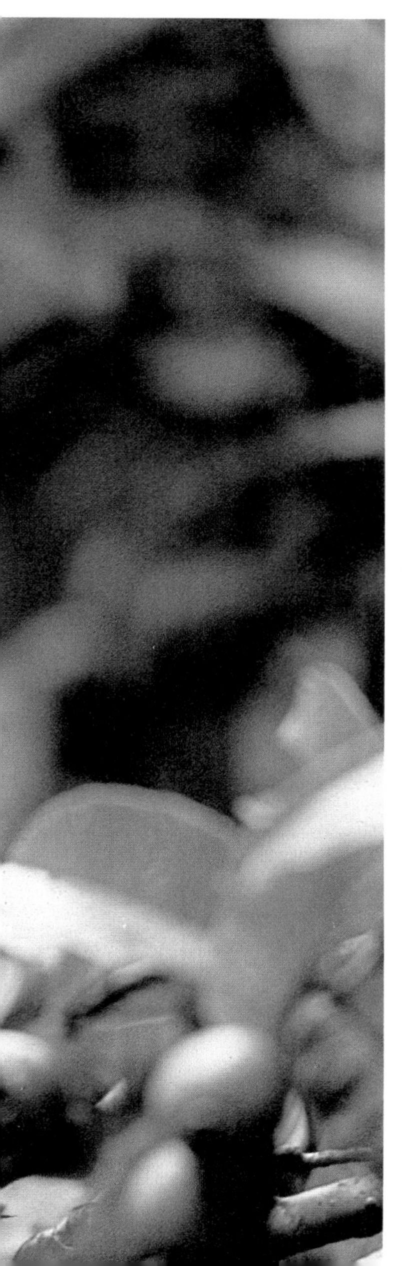

Iguanas and Other Lizards

Still other reptiles live both in the trees and in the water. One of these is the iguana, which is easily spotted on tree branches. Often these lizards fall victim to Indians who hunt them from their pirogues, unless the iguanas can jump into the water in time. Thanks to their long legs and sturdy toes, they can move swiftly both in the water and on dry land. They lay oval eggs on sandbanks that form on the rivers after the floods retreat. These eggs are a source of food for the people of the Amazon who regularly harvest them. Iguanas are a good example of adaptation to the two main habitats of Amazonia—water and forest.

The tropical South American forests have numerous species of lizards. Some of them are small, not much longer than a few inches, and dwell on the layer of leaves and plant matter that accumulates on the forest floor. Like other small animals of the forest (amphibians, snakes, insects, scorpions, and millipedes), they seek shelter inside the tufts of a thorny palm tree *(Astrocaryum paramaca)*. They come out into the open to hunt prey proportionate to their size. They particularly like springtails, which are very primitive insects that feed on plant matter. Other lizards are larger and dwell in the various layers of the Amazonian forest. Among

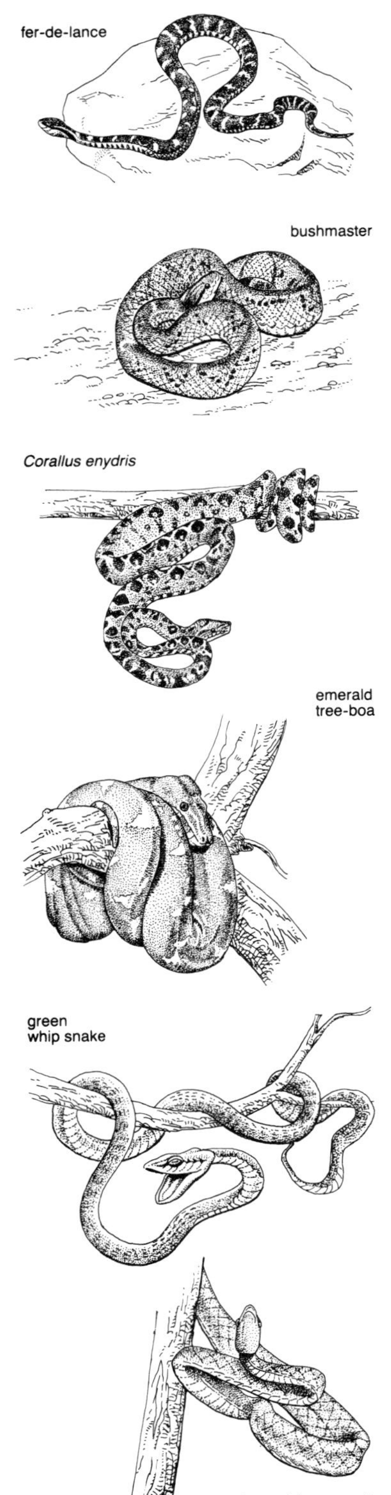

them are geckos and some members of the family Iguanidae, which have a wide variety of shapes and sizes.

Many members of the family Teidae, Amazonia's ecological counterparts to North American lizards, can modify their color. Some are very tiny and inhabit the layer of dead leaves on the forest floor. Others, of larger size, live in the trees and feed on insects, fruit, and leaves.

Harmless and Poisonous Snakes

Few people have never heard of the snakes of the great Amazon jungle. In this region, with its invariably hot and humid climate and its wealth of prey, snakes have evolved into many highly differentiated species. They have also come to play a part in the legends that surround the Amazon.

The most legendary species is surely the anaconda, an aquatic species that shares the river environment with several others. The aquatic snakes of the Amazon are all viviparous or ovoviviparous. In the latter case, the female incubates the eggs within her body and lays them when they are ready to hatch.

The anaconda has been the source of many legends, especially where its size is concerned. Some authors of the past would have us believe that the anaconda can reach lengths of as much as 72 feet (22 m). In reality, scientific measurements suggest a maximum length of 39 feet (12 m). The anaconda lives mainly in the water or within its immediate vicinity. It feeds on both aquatic and land animals such as amphibians, fish, turtles, capybaras, tapirs, and water birds.

The female anaconda delivers from fourteen to eighty-two young, each 30 inches (75 cm) long and weighing 7 ounces (200 gm). In one year, the young will double their length; in three, they will be 10 feet (3 m) long. After this, their growth will proceed more slowly.

The snakes of most concern to people in the Amazon forest are the poisonous ones. Fortunately, there are not many. The most common are in the family Crotalidae, in particular *Bothrops atrox*.

This snake is distinguished by its massive body terminating in a pointed tail and for its large triangular head. Slightly longer in length is the bushmaster (Lachesis muta), which is another very similar species. These snakes are especially active at night but may also be found during the day. They blend easily into the thick vegetation because of

A young anaconda with its rather slender body is easily recognized by its characteristic coloration. This snake is only one representative of the family Boidae (boa) that today is entirely aquatic. The anaconda, together with the jaguar, constitutes the main threat posed to humans by large vertebrates in the vast Amazonian forest.

their coloring--gray, cream, or yellow with pronounced dark triangles. Their poison is destructive to both red blood cells and the nervous system. A lethal dose for a person is 10 milligrams. The amount in the snake's poison glands is between 20 and 40 milligrams.

Other poisonous serpents include coral snakes, which have long bodies, small rounded heads, and sequences of black, white, and red rings. They are extremely poisonous, and a single bite can be fatal to a person.

Other Amazonian serpents are harmless to people. Among these, both tree- and land-dwelling boas kill their animal prey by suffocation. The very slender thread snake of the family Leptotyphlopidae lives on the ground or in the branches of low trees and are not a threat to humans. The vine snakes of the genera *Leptophis* and *Oxybelis* live entirely in the trees where they hunt lizards and small mammals.

THE FOREST MANTLE

Opposite page: In the Amazon forest, vegetation is made up of trees and only 20 percent grasses. The grasses have to be well adapted to the dim light under the tree canopy in order to survive. On the other hand, they have no trouble finding water.This element is readily available throughout the year, sometimes in excessive quantities. For this reason, many plants in Amazonia have adapted so as to withstand flooding, but none has particularly strong defenses against drought.

A constant high temperature throughout the year, water in great quantities, and sufficient atmospheric humidity are optimum conditions for the growth of lush vegetation. Practically the entire area of Amazonia has a covering of green. It extends into the Guyanese forests with basic similarities in composition and form. South America is endowed with a splendid forest that runs from the Andean slopes to the coasts of Guyana and northern Brazil. Minor exceptions are the coastal savannas and some stretches of the interior.

Formation and Shape

The *Hylea Amazonica*, as Humboldt called it, represents the largest forested area in the world. It extends across 1.14 billion acres (460 million hectares) in Brazil alone. It has both ancient and modern roots. The ancient roots date back to the Tertiary period. The modern ones are due to rapid climatic changes over the course of several brief geological periods. Alternating periods of drought pushed the forest toward the wetlands of the west and the Guyanese plains.

Flying over the Amazon, the forest appears homogeneous (of a uniform structure). An infinite canopy of tree foliage in which all shades of green are mixed is interrupted here and there by colorful patches of trees in blossom. Going down the river, the forest appears as a great growing wall draped in vines and aerial roots. This uniformity is an illusion. The forest, in fact, changes from east to west according to the nature of the soil and microclimatic conditions—climatic conditions within a locally defined area. These factors are more variable than they might appear.

Outlaws of the Forest

Amazon forest vegetation consists mainly of tree species. Arboreal (tree) species make up 80 percent of this vegetation. The remaining 20 percent is represented by herbaceous (soft, nonwood) plants. The trees and bushes are always green, even when a few individuals lose some or all of their leaves. An uninterrupted green cover prevents almost all the sun's light from reaching the forest floor. Only on the banks of rivers, in natural or artificial clearings, or wherever a great tree has been uprooted does the sun touch soil. It is here that the youngest and most fragile plants find a way to reach light.

Another characteristic of this forest is its incredible

This drawing shows the spread of the large rain forests throughout Amazonia, Guyana, and the surrounding territories. These forests follow the flow of the large rivers, forming corridors that adjoin deciduous forests and dry savannas. Some savannas are found in the very heart of Amazonia, in the region of the upper reaches of the Branco River, and in the area of the llanos in the Orinoco Basin of Venezuela. On the map, the Andes mountain range is marked in black.

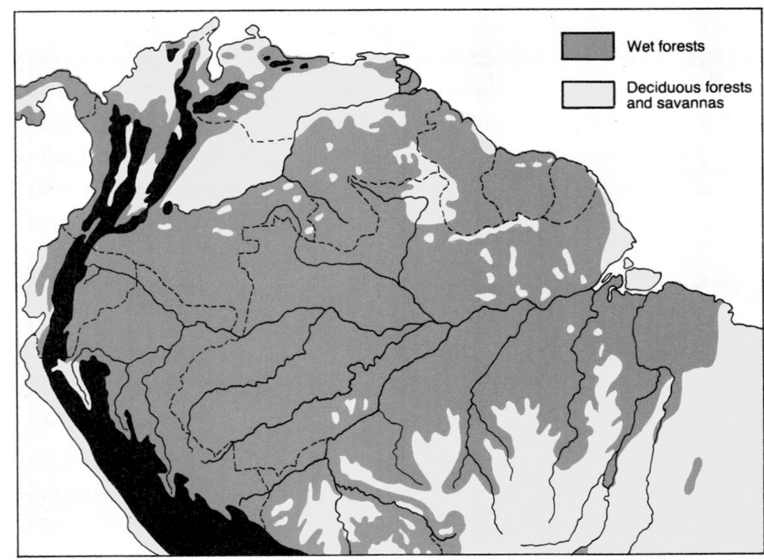

diversity. In temperate forests, one species usually dominates. Here, however, a marvelous variety is distributed throughout the forest, apparently without any clear pattern. This situation makes the harvest of economically desirable trees very difficult, given that they are not easily located when in the midst of other, unusable species.

Many censuses have been taken of vegetation in the Amazon. All of them are revealing. In a region near Manaus, 110 species with trunk diameters of over 1 inch (2.5 cm) were counted within an area of about 385 sq. miles (1,000 sq. km). Elsewhere, in another area of the same size, botanists counted 423 trees belonging to 87 different species. The figures become astronomically high if the total plant population is taken into consideration. Three thousand plant species have been identified in an area of 1 sq. mile (2.5 sq. km). These are enormous numbers when compared with those of the temperate forests.

A Multilayered Forest

Over most of the Amazon forest, large trees form an unbroken cover about 130 feet (40 m) above the ground. Botanists distinguish several horizons, or horizontal layers, demonstrating that the structure of the forest is more complex and better organized than it seems at first glance.

Ground vegetation is scarce, as sunlight barely reaches the lowest horizon. In the dim light under leaf cover, the most decorative plants grow. These are arums, with di-

The Peruvian Amazon forest is seen from an airplane. A river curves nearly full circle, almost enclosing a stretch of forest. If the narrow isthmus, not quite visible at the lower edge of the picture, is washed away during a flood, the loop of water will be isolated from the main course of the river. The area will then become a swamp.

versely colored central spadixes (central shafts housing flower clusters), begonias, philodendrons, and monsteras with fringed leaves. Under the shade of these plants, only young seedlings and some grasses can grow.

The middle horizon is made of bushes and young trees that are trying to make their way toward the sunlight in between their older kin. Here, especially in the humid areas, numerous palm trees and ferns are found.

Above everything else, the horizon of tree foliage rising up on straight trunks is dominant. At the base of trees are adventitious roots (roots that originate from branches) and spurs. They seem to buttress trees above the ground, adding to the support of their trunks. The first main branches emerge from the trunks at a height of about 80 feet (25 m). Some giants outgrow the general cover and their foliage can develop up to as high as 200 feet (60 m). Their appearance

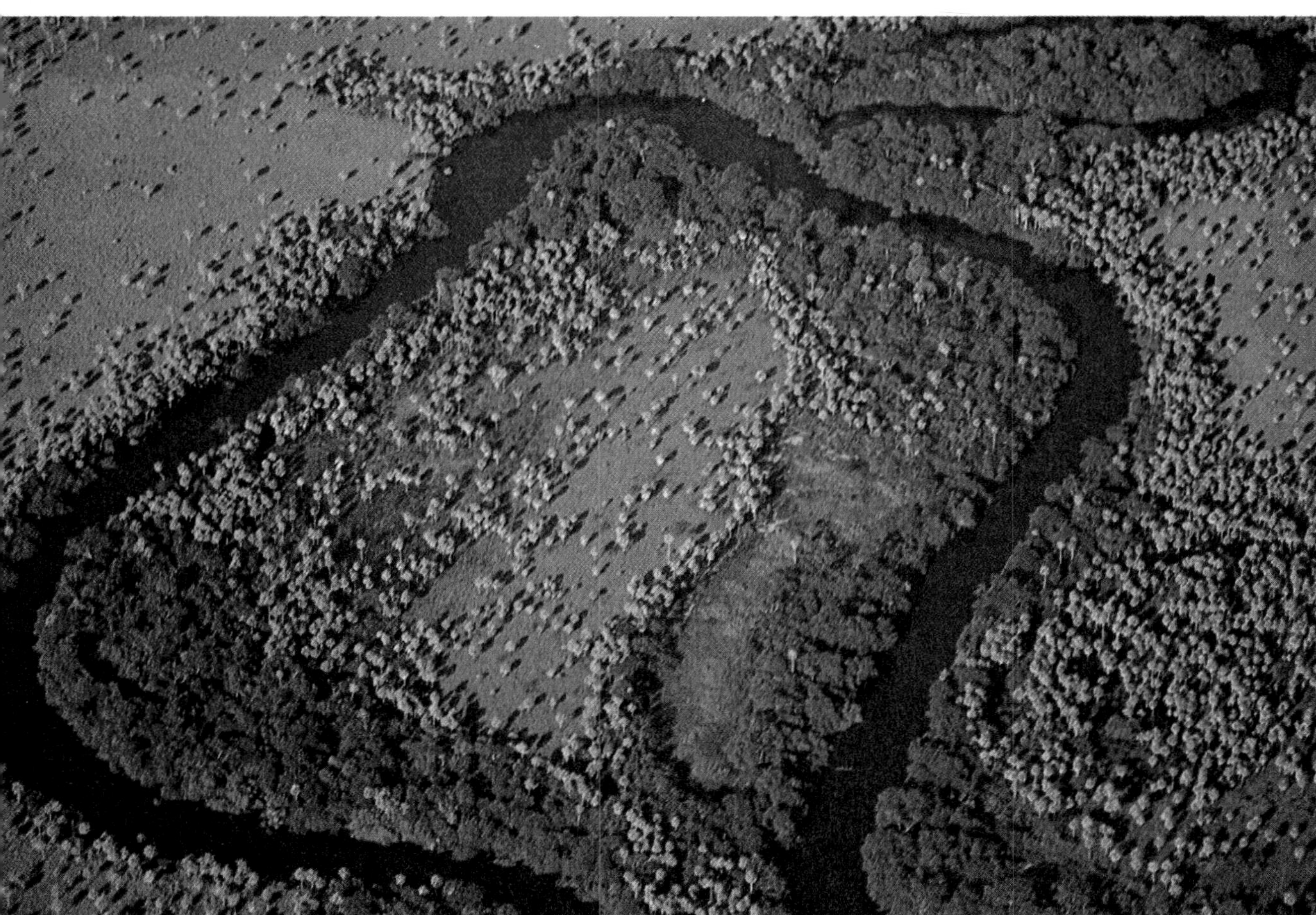

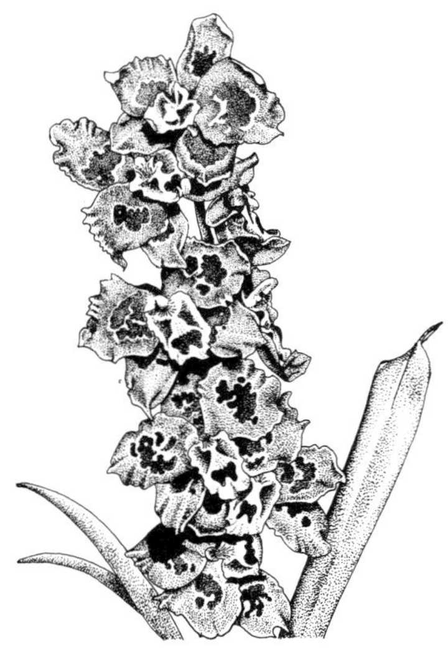

dominates all vegetation of the entire forest.

At times, the use of these horizons to group plants together is not a very efficient method. Vines, for example, escape every kind of classification. They grow throughout the entire forest cover and cannot be confined to any of the horizons. At their base, they can be the size of a human body. In order to climb up to the forest canopy, they must cling to the trunks of other trees. When they find enough light, they produce leaves and sometimes beautiful flowers. Some vines grow as straight as a taut rope. Others twist on the ground, taking on surreal shapes. Many of them use trees only as support, but some can be very harmful to the trees to which they cling.

Many epiphytic plants also inhabit the Amazon forest. Like vines, they use the trunks of large trees. Unlike vines, they are never parasitic. They are numerous throughout the area, but most are found on the forested mountain slopes on the Atlantic side of Brazil. Among them are various orchids with their clusters of brightly colored and unusually shaped flowers.

Unexpectedly, some cacti also dwell in the Amazon forest. Young plants of the genus *Rhipsalis* are spiny, while adult plants have harmless thorns bent downward.

Ferns are also numerous. As a result of a long period of evolution, these plants have adapted to a very peculiar environment. They have learned to withstand both excessive humidity and excessive dryness. They use only their roots to cling to the trees. They absorb all nutrients, water, and minerals, directly from the atmosphere. The leaves at the base of the plant form a type of bowl. All of the leaves are coated with a waxy layer that prevents evaporation and desiccation (drying up). Under this wax, there is a layer of cells loaded with water, as in aquatic plants. The epiphytic plants of the Amazon forest, especially those belonging to the family Bromeliaceae, are half way between xerophytic plants (those preferring dry environments) and aquatic plants. Thus, they can survive in an environment in which rain alternates with dry periods. All of them have wonderful leaves and flowers of extraordinary shapes and colors.

Many Types of Forest

The Brazilian people divide the huge forests into three categories according to the amount of water in the soil. Some areas are permanently under the water. Others are covered with water only during flooding. Still others are always dry.

Tropical orchids are so beautiful that they have triggered, with some collectors, a destructive frenzy. The pickers may even cut down the trees where they grow in the effort to obtain them, thus causing serious damage. In Colombia, one picker alone managed to assemble about ten thousand plants of *Odontoglossum crispum* by cutting down four thousand trees. This drastically reduced the chances of survival for this particular plant.

This strangler fig is already an adult at the last stage of its growth. Inside its trunk is a hollow area. It is the spot where the unfortunate plant the fig used as its support used to be. The remains of this plant have completely disappeared, destroyed by fungi, bacteria, and small, wood-eating animals.

Distribution of the forests is determined by areas of periodic flooding. The so-called forests of terra firma grow only upon land that is never flooded. It contrasts with the igapos and várzeas which develop in areas flooded for varied periods throughout the year. The rivers sometimes overrun their beds for great distances. The beds are thus flanked in some places by banks upon which, with the passage of time, human populations have established dwellings, farms, and grazing lands.

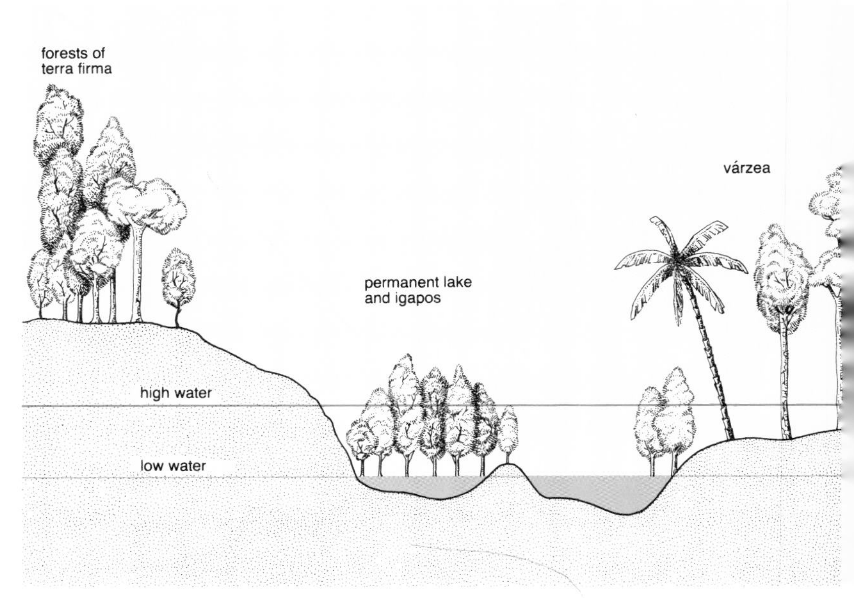

Plant species and shapes vary in these three environments.

The first type of forest, called "igapós" by the Brazilians, is swamp forest permanently flooded by water. During some parts of the dry season, however, the water level retreats, and expanses of mud are left behind. The underbrush of the igapós is rich in bushes, palm trees, and ferns, which grow among the trees. These trees are often buttressed by spurs that ensure a strong hold on the highly unstable ground. They are much shorter than their relatives living on dry land. Among the most common species are the jacareuba, the arapari, the abiurana, and the *louros do igapó* (a Brazilian term referring to the environment colonized by this plant). Vines are rare, but epiphytic plants abound, taking advantage of the exceptional humidity. The second type of forest is that of the várzeas. These areas are covered by water during the annual flooding of the large rivers. Sometimes they surround the river for only several yards, but often they stretch for miles, depending on the level reached by the water. In this environment, palm trees abound. For example, there is the pachiuba, which is supported on special shoots, or "stilts." Small *Geonema* palms are so spiny that they make exploration of the area impossible. Pinots palms, on the other hand, are famous because their cores are harvested to produce palm hearts, a prized delicacy. The trees of the forest, which usually do not exceed 65 to 100 feet

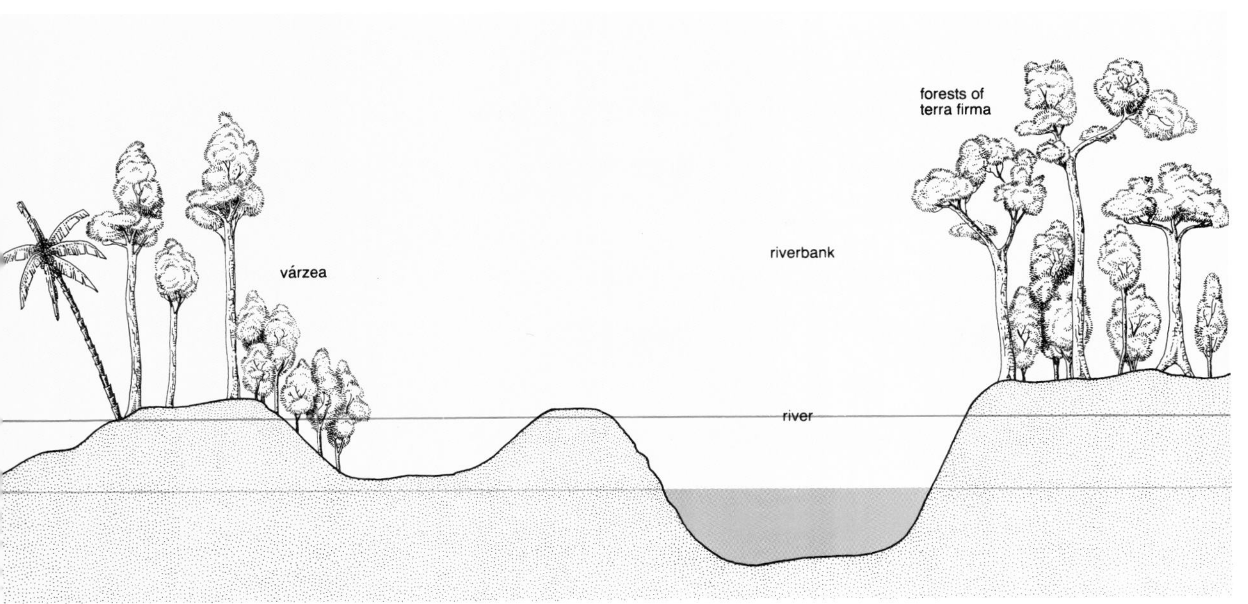

(20 to 30 m), are highly varied. Among them are found oeirana, imbauba, tachis, mutamba, assacu, and pau mulato. Hevea plants and abundant vines also thrive.

These swampy or temporarily underwater forests cover wide surfaces. The area that the várzeas covers is 25,096 sq. miles (65,000 sq km), one and a half times the surface of the Netherlands. As the level of the soil rises, the várzeas give way to the forests of terra firma. These forests are very rich in plant life, especially arboreal species. There are acapus, pau amarelo, pausanto, massarandubas, jaranas, matamatas, and many others. There are also some palms, especially the urucuri, that highlight the exotic character of these territories.

The majestic forest, with trees that reach dizzying heights, is also populated with the most extraordinary animals in the Amazon.

The Useful Plants

The Amazon is rich in plants of great commercial interest. Among these, the best known are those that serve in the production of India rubber. When he returned from America, Christopher Columbus recounted that some Indian tribes shaped balls out of a sort of blackish gum that had strange properties. The natives called this substance *cahuchu*, which means "crying tree."

A huge tree in the Amazon forest is seen from below. The Amazon is rich in commercially valuable plants, such as *Hevea*, which produces India rubber, cocoa, *Mauritia flexuosa*, and others. It is certain that many useful plants, as yet unknown, are disappearing as the forests are destroyed. It is also certain that unknown species outnumber known species by far.

There are several plant species that produce this substance and are called rubber trees. The bully tree produces a milky liquid that coagulates to form balata, the material used in the manufacture of golf balls. The most important trees in rubber production are the Hevea trees, various species of which live in Amazonia. The most valuable of these is *Hevea brasiliensis*, which grows almost exclusively on the right bank of the Amazon River. On the left bank, a similar species replaces it. These Euphorbiaceae, as tall as 100 feet (30 m), are rich in latex.

The list of plants that are useful to people include many palms. The babassu is not typical of the Amazon forest but grows mainly at the boundary of the province of Maranhão. It has also been planted in various other zones of Brazil. It is a slender palm with decorative leaves and large egglike fruits. These fruits contain a pit from which an oil similar to coconut oil can be extracted. Another palm, already mentioned, is the buruti. It has many uses. Its fruit is edible, and its sap can be made into palm wine. Bread can be made from its core. Fishing nets, hammocks, and ropes are woven from its fibers. The leaves of the buruti are useful as roofing material, and its wood as lumber for construction of houses.

Amid the humid underbrush grow the cocoa plant and the castanheira, which produces Brazil nuts. One vine of the family Sapindaceae, *Paullinia cupana*, produces the seeds that are the basis of guarana, one of the national drinks of Brazil. The Amazon is also renowned for the production of timber used in construction work and for fine carvings. The angelim, the cedra rana, and many acajous are some of the more famous plants.

The Indians know the properties of plants much better than the Europeans or the North Americans. They make use of them in a variety of ways. *Strychnos toxifera*, for example, is a bush whose roots produce an extremely potent poison called "curare." The Indians extract a powder from these plants and soak it in water. Concentrated by boiling, this liquid becomes a thick brown paste to which they add other poisons extracted from frogs or toads. Curare contains a strong alkaloid, an organic base containing nitrogen and, usually, oxygen. It acts on the nerve endings of warm-blooded animals to cause cramps, asphyxiation, and, eventually, death. The Indians use this poison in fishing, hunting, and war. Arrows dipped in curare are launched with bows or blowguns. The poison paralyzes prey in a few minutes.

Chemists have isolated the active substance of the plant, which is used in small doses to treat tetanus and epilepsy.

Savannas at the Edges of the Forests

Here and there, across the expanse of the Amazon, traces of major fragmentation that occurred during the dry periods of the Pleistocene epoch can be seen. The nature of the soil—for example that of the ancient geological shield in Guyana—is not always favorable to the growth of lush vegetation.

There are some hills called "inselbergs" on which the rock is completely bare, or covered by only a thin layer of soil that might be colonized by plants. Here, the large forest trees disappear and are replaced by thinner plants and low, bushy vegetation. The plants acquire a typically xerophytic appearance, which is surprising in the heart of a humid forest. Some of these hills are inhabited by Indians, who

A large *Hevea* plant stands in the wilderness of the Xingu region of the Amazon forest. The cuts that are visible were made by latex collectors. Today, collection of latex in the wilds has practically disappeared. It has been replaced by the cultivation of selected plants and by the production of synthetic rubber.

The shadow of a DC3 falls upon a wide savanna in the middle of the Amazon forest. From a plane, it is very easy to distinguish savanna areas from the rain forest. Clouds disperse above the savannas, and it is possible to clearly see the features of the underlying territory.

find the living conditions better there. They are on drier land and are protected from enemies that are easier to sight from the hills.

The most interesting savannas, which are grasslands scattered with trees or shrubs, are those that break up the forests in the region of the Branco River's upper reaches. These savannas seem to be connected with the dry expanses of southeastern Brazil and with the llanos, or plains, of the Orinoco. They are what remains of the long corridor of savanna that crossed this region during the dry periods of the Pleistocene epoch. Here, there is less rainfall and a well-marked dry season in which the trees shed all of their leaves. Seen from a plane, the contrast is obvious. The clouds of the tropical forests disappear, leaving clear blue sky. A partial forest with low trees and a savanna covered with grasses appear. The bare and sandy ground is evidence that the permeable nature of the soil has combined with climatic features to create unexpected dry islands in the very middle of the wet forest. Also, the savanna is continually gaining ground because of fires started by cattle ranchers.

INSECTS AND SPIDERS

Opposite page: In the Amazon forest, bumblebees construct their huge and complex nests (like that in the picture) with a substance similar to papier mâché. Beside bumblebees and wasps, many species of bees also inhabit the area. Their honey is traditionally harvested by the Indians as well as by some animals that are not bothered by their stings. Some bee species typical of Africa and introduced in America, especially in Guyana, have turned unusually aggressive. This is a radical change from their behavior in their home country, the reasons for which are not yet known.

In the Amazon, there are a surprising number of species of insects and arthropods (spiders). In 1848, Henry Bates left England for the Amazon with Alfred Wallace. After two months, he had sent back to the British Museum in London over thirteen hundred different insects, all collected around the village of Pará. Bates spent eleven years in the Amazon and collected over fourteen thousand species of insects. Of these, over seven thousand had never been described before. More recently, 150 different species of mosquitoes were counted in the Colombian Amazon. Also, seven hundred different species of butterflies were found around Belém and five hundred species around Ega. Nevertheless, entomologists (scientists who study insects) believe that we know only one-third or one-fourth of the total number of species existing in the Amazon.

A Myriad of Insects

Some insect species are present in the tens of millions of individuals and play an important role in the biological balances of the forest. Other species are not easily found, not even in museums. Perhaps these insects are particularly difficult to find because they live at the level of the treetops or simply because their populations are sparse.

Not all insects of the Amazon are on good terms with humans. Huge numbers of mosquitoes, for example, are a problem at some times of the year. Some minute flies, even worse than the mosquitoes, dwell in the humid forests. They include black flies and others belonging to the family Ceratopogonidae.

Various species of wasps, bees, and bumblebees are also found. Some of the insects belonging to the family Pompilidae found in South America have a wingspan up to 5 inches (12 cm). Their wings and body are an intense metallic blue or purple color. They feed mainly on spiders, especially tarantulas. The relationship between predator and prey is very curious. These insects kill spiders with a fast-acting poison. Then they build a shelter for it and lay one egg on top. In this way, the growing insect larva will have a plentiful supply of fresh food.

The incredible variation of insects in this humid forest has been documented by recent studies. Heretofore neglected insect groups have been identified. The Acridae are represented by an enormous number of species, and all these species play an important role in the ecological balance of the forest.

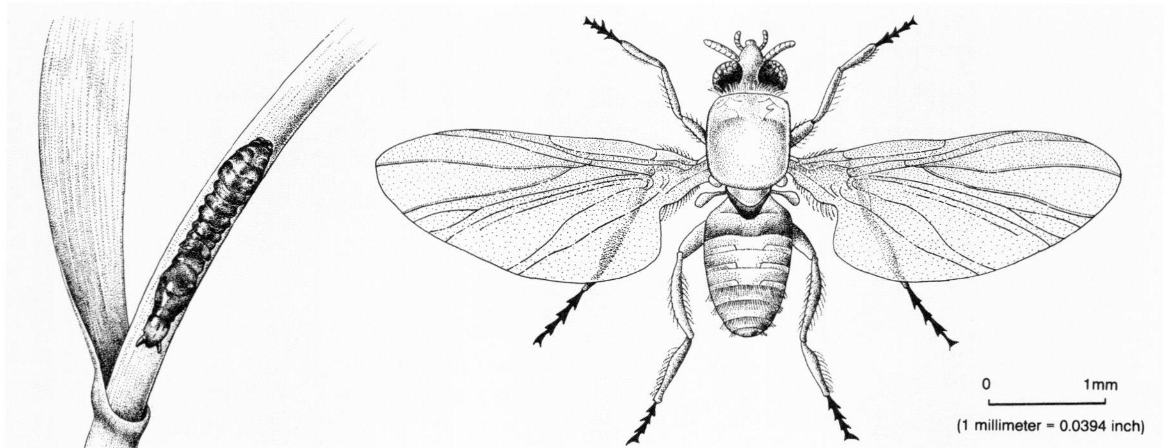

The black flies, shown in this picture in larval and adult forms, are very tiny with iridescent wings. The mouth of the female is modified for biting mammals and sucking their blood. These modifications are not found in the male. The females need blood in order to aid in the maturation of their eggs. Numerous species of black flies can sometimes gather in huge swarms. At times they are a real scourge, both in Amazonia and in other regions of the world. Their bite is very painful, and, due to their small size, they can pass through most mosquito netting. Moreover, this species can transmit various illnesses and parasites.

Ants

In forest life, ants play an important role as recyclers of organic matter. They are also a fundamental link in many food chains. The number of ant species in the Amazon is very high, and each species has a specific feeding pattern. Some are vegetarians, like the leaf-eating ants called "saubas" by the Brazilians. These belong to the Attini group and are easily recognized by their habit of walking on the leaf-covered ground in long columns.

Carnivorous ant species are also found in Amazonia. The most well known are the army ants that, unlike other species, are almost exclusively nomadic. They only settle in a given locality for reproduction. Army ants are ferocious predators that devour all the animals in their way. Their prey includes insects, small vertebrates, frogs, and some lizards that the ants find by probing the holes and cracks in trees. Their bites are very painful. Indians will evacuate their villages when they see the ants coming and wait for them to move on.

Army ants do not build anthills. During their nomadic periods, they settle every day in different locations, seeking shelter under logs and rocks. There, the workers form a sort of structure with their bodies. In the middle of this living shelter, their queen resides. During the nomadic period, she is not yet heavy with eggs. The number of ants can climb to a million individuals. During the move, some workers bear larvae and others hunt for food. When the larvae have completed their development and are ready to undergo metamorphosis into pupae (the cocoon stage), the group stops. Within a week the queen starts laying eggs. After eight days, twenty-five thousand eggs hatch all at once. The colony, now made up of young workers (the larvae of the previous generation) and newborn larvae, can resume nomadic life. It sets off in search of prey necessary to satisfy its insatiable appetite. The life of these ants, therefore, is a rhythmic succession of forced marches and rests, which is related to the reproductive cycle of the queen.

Many birds feed selectively upon ants. One family, the Formicaridae, has taken its name from this habit. Some species of mammals, such as anteaters have also specialized in ant-catching. Some tree-dwelling anteaters search for their prey on tree branches, while others, like the giant anteater capture them on the ground.

The workers of the leaf-eating ants carry leaf fragments, often much larger than themselves. They move in single file on their way to the ant nest. There, other workers will transport the leaves to large chambers and turn them into a foamy paste that they spread on the ground. In this "fertilized field," they will grow highly specialized fungi. There is a peculiar association between insects and plants. Both larvae and adults feed on this fungus, whose growth seems to be accelerated by the saliva of the workers. Over 600,000 individuals inhabit each ant nest. Because of their incredible appetite, the workers must explore wider and wider stretches of forest. If they get into cultivated farmland, they can cause irreparable damage.

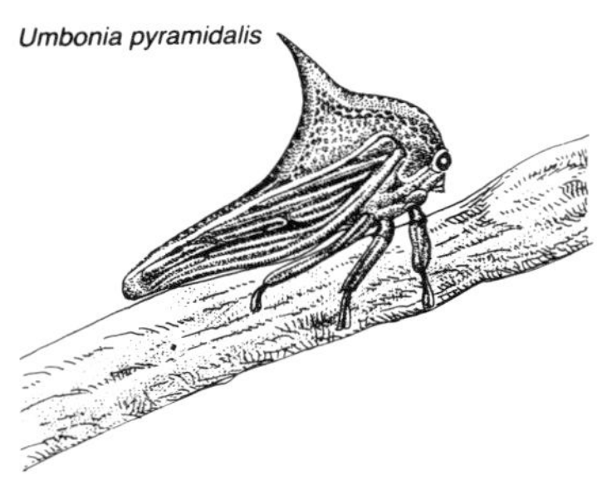

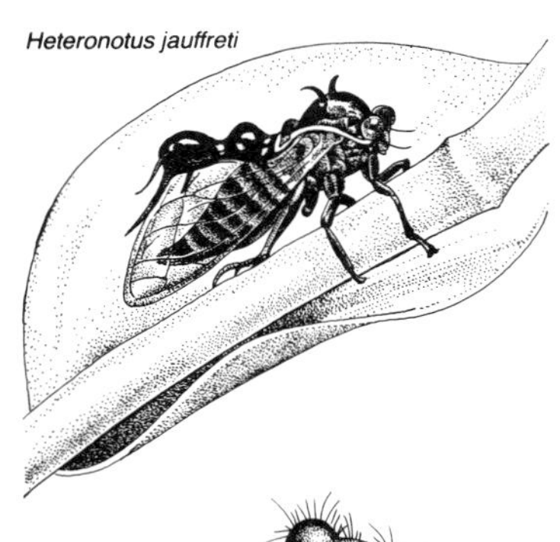

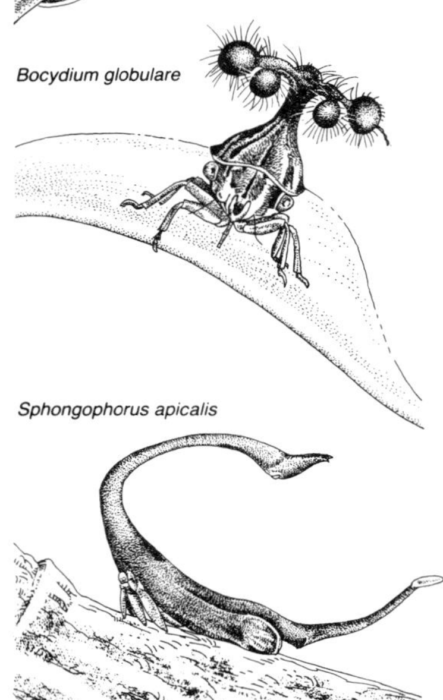

The size of treehoppers may vary between 0.2 and 0.6 inches (5 and 15 mm). They can be found on leaves and branches. The front section of their bodies is often crowned with bizarre protuberances such as spikes, globes, and other strange elongations bent back over the abdomen. All appear to be useless appendages. These insects seem to have emerged from the imagination of an artist.

Termites

It would take a great time to examine the life cycle of termites in detail, but it is impossible to skip over them entirely. These tiny, social insects are highly specialized. They are never longer than 0.6 inches (15 mm) and are usually much smaller. Termites play a basic role in the forest, and in the recycling of organic matter. Together with the larvae of wood-eating beetles, they are the primary consumers of wood.

Many termites live in trees, and their huge, multi-tunneled nests can be seen everywhere. For most of their life cycle, they cannot stand sunlight. Other species live on the ground. All of them are organized in strict hierarchical societies numbering millions of individuals. These are divided into three castes: sexually active individuals, soldiers, and workers. These castes are, in turn, divided into subcastes, each one with precisely defined functions. Termites will attack anything made of wood. For this reason, they can be a serious problem for humans in the Amazon and other warm regions.

Treehoppers and Lantern Flies

In the Amazon, there are some peculiar insects that are related to cicadas. These include treehoppers (family Membracidae). This family is also found in Europe, and it is very well represented in South America. Half of the twenty-five hundred species known to entomologists today live in the Amazon.

Lantern flies (family Fulgoridae) are closely related to the treehoppers. They are larger and have very strange shapes. Some lantern flies have heads shaped like those of alligators. This seems a useless feature in an animal barely an inch long. Scientists have theorized that these animals give off light during the night. However, this peculiarity has not yet been verified. The glow may be a result of the occasional presence of light-generating bacteria on the insect's head. For whatever reason, they have been given the name lantern fly.

Beetles

The Amazon hosts many members of beetle families typical of the tropics. A great many species are well known for the beauty of their carapaces, their extraordinary shapes, and their interesting behavior. The long-horned beetle group is well represented by numerous species. Usually

Euchroma gigantea

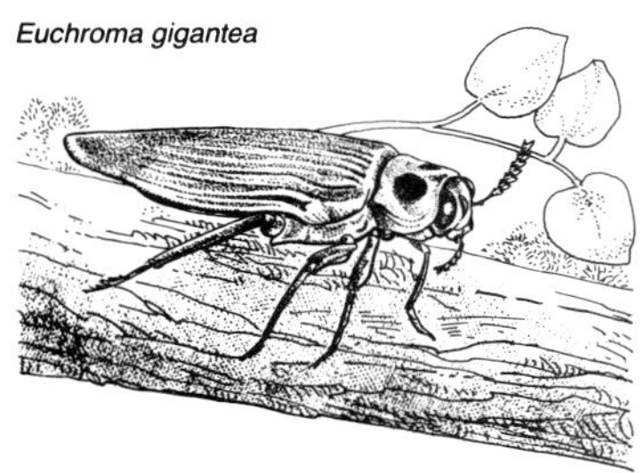

Oxsternon festivum

Erotylus

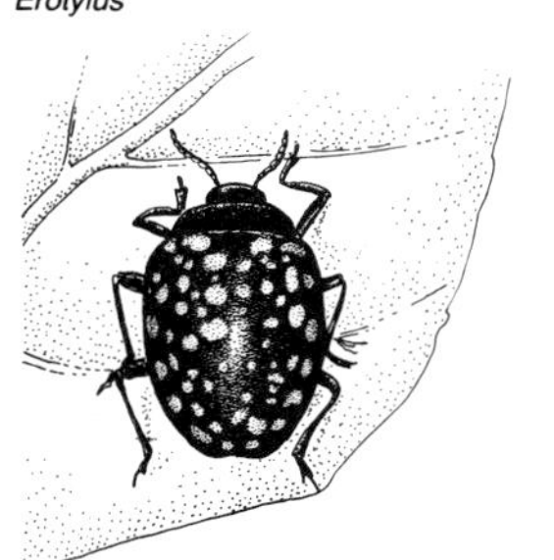

Dynastes hercules

Many Amazonian beetles are very small. Some can be gigantic, such as the rhinoceros beetle, which can grow to be 6 inches (15 cm) long. The male is equipped with a horn that can reach 2.3 inches (6 cm) long. Along with Titanus giganteus, this is the largest insect in the world. It is curious to note that Amazonia also hosts hummingbirds, some of which are not longer than several inches.

they are small, but sometimes they can be as long as 5 inches (12 cm). Their wing covers are often adorned with beautiful black, brown, and white patterns. This provides them with excellent camouflage on the bark of the trees in which they live.

Other interesting beetles are the fireflies, which belong to the family Lampyridae. These beetles have light-producing organs throughout all stages of their growth, including the larval stage. Their light is produced by a chemical reaction that occurs between specific substances within the light-producing organ. At dusk, charming dances, sometimes performed by males and females and at other times by males alone, can be seen.

Many other beetles deserve mention for their astounding beauty. Among them the Cetonidae and Crisomelidae are found in small groups on flowers and leaves. They are often tiny. When examined under a magnifying glass, they resemble gold inlaid with jewels and precious stones. The Buprestidae are sturdy-looking, elongated beetles ornamented with the brightest metallic colorations.

Butterflies

The Amazon teems with butterflies. Some species are discovered only after close observation. The colors and patterns on the wings of the Geometridae and Noctuidae render them almost invisible when they land on tree trunks. Other species, belonging to the family Tirididae, resemble leaves—even to the point of imitating veins, fungal patches, and holes. Most of the species belonging to the family Amatidae inhabit South America. These butterflies can be mistaken for wasps. They imitate wasps through the use of their transparent wings and elongated bodies that narrow at the abdomen. The lower side of the wings of many butterflies has a coloration similar to that of plants. These butterflies are, therefore, very hard to spot when they are at rest. In flight, however, they light up in an explosion of color.

Many other species have bright colorations. In order to see them one need only wait beside a blossoming bush or along a trail beside a muddy pool. Water attracts them in huge numbers. They belong to numerous families, some widespread throughout the tropical regions, others found only in America. Among the latter group is the family Eliconiidae, which numbers about one hundred species. All of them have a wingspan of between 2.5 to 3.5 inches (6 to 9 cm) and exceedingly rich coloration.

The picture very clearly shows the extraordinary differences between the sexes of a spider of the genus *Argiopes*. The female's body is as wide as the entire male with its legs outstretched *(here shown above her in the picture)*. Another interesting feature of this species is its habit of diving under the water, which is a convenient adaptation in such a wet environment.

Certainly no butterfly can compete with the sumptuous *Morpho*. The males are a bright metallic blue color while the females have a more modest coloration. These insects fly with very slow pulses of their wings. Nevertheless, they sail swiftly and safely, through clearings and along trails of the forest. Butterfly hunters attract them with boards covered with metallic blue paper. This deceives the males into thinking that they are encountering rivals. Stories are told of forest rangers who have worn bright blue plastic helmets that glitter in the sun. They have become surrounded by Morpho butterflies that had come fluttering out from the forest. The wingspan can be as wide as 7 inches (18 cm), and sometimes their sparkle can be seen from a low-flying airplane. The caterpillars of this species are covered with stinging hairs. They undergo metamorphosis in a cocoon that is sometimes woven collectively by more than one larva.

Many interesting cases of mimicry (resemblance of an animal or plant to its surroundings for the purpose of protection) are seen among Amazon butterflies. Some species are completely harmless but can imitate to perfection the shapes, colors, and movement of other species thought to be toxic. Toxicity in the imitated species can be due to chemi-

cals ingested by their caterpillars or to secretions of special glands. These secretions are repellent to potential predators. This is an example of parallel evolution between two distantly related groups living in the same habitat. Henry Bates has studied this phenomenon in particular detail. For this reason this form of imitation is called "Batesian Mimicry." For example, many species of the family Eliconiidae markedly imitate species of the family Danaidae, which are usually very brightly colored. Sometimes the imitation of wing shapes and patterns is so perfect that only in-depth anatomical studies allow scientists to distinguish the mimetic species from the original. Here, the imitating species takes advantage of safety from predators enjoyed by the toxic or repellent species.

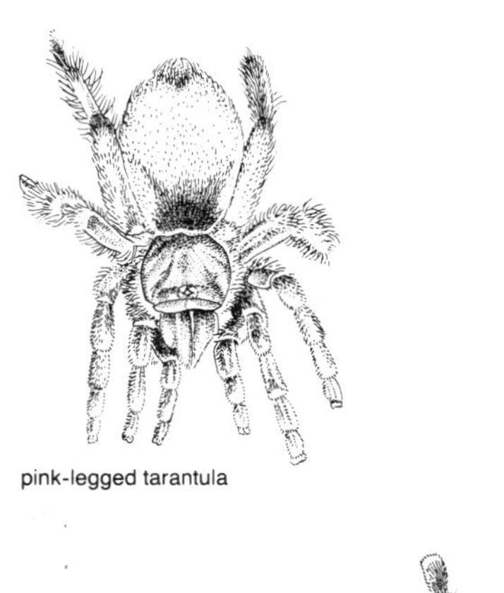

pink-legged tarantula

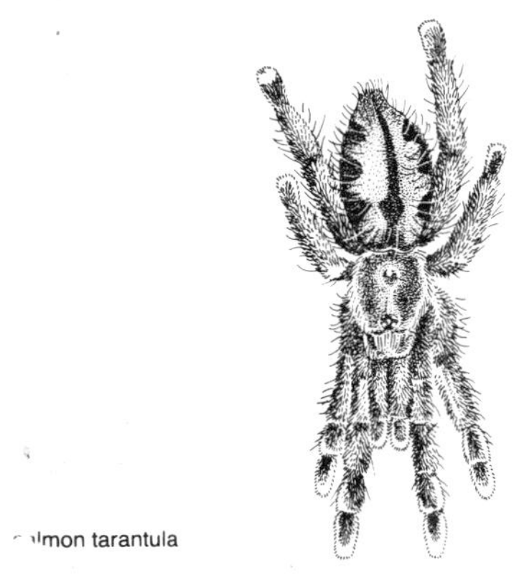

lmon tarantula

Spiders

The beauty of insects exists side by side with the intrigue of a great many spiders that also inhabit the forest. Each species has its own domain, whether on the ground, in the bushes, or in large trees. They spin webs of highly varied shapes and dimensions, some of which are geometric works of art. All of the spiders are carnivores that feed mainly on living prey.

The most infamous spider is the tarantula. Tarantulas are widespread throughout warm regions all over the world. They are especially abundant in tropical America. The body of some species can be about 4 inches (10 cm) long, but the total size is increased considerably by their very long legs, and by the blackish hairs which give them a repellent appearance. In some species, the tips of the legs are red, in contrast to a black body.

Smaller spiders feed on insects, millipedes, sow bugs, and other spiders. Larger tarantulas attack small vertebrates such as amphibians, lizards, snakes, small mammals, and sometimes even birds. Hummingbirds have been seen in the process of being caught and devoured by such spiders.

Spiders kill their prey with a poison, which they inject through their cheliceras (first pair of appendages near the mouth). They can be dangerous to people, even though most members of the species do not bite humans and do not have deadly poison. Spiders belonging to the genus *Lycosa* have poisons that can cause serious gangrene and even tissue decomposition. However, there are serums that can counteract these poisons. They are available in regions of high risk.

Some tarantulas, called carpenter tarantulas, spend most of their lives on the ground. There, they dig their burrows that are often closed by a makeshift door. Other smaller species live on the bushes at the bases of trees, keeping to the edges of large webs and waiting for their prey. The real giants of this group are tree dwellers that build short silk tubes for their homes. Still other large-sized species live on the ground, hiding in their burrows during the day but emerging during the evening to hunt. The females of this species can live to be twenty years old. The danger of these species to humans must not be overrated.

BIRDS

South America has been nicknamed "the continent of the birds." This name is justified by the presence of a wealth of birds that is unique in the world. Undoubtedly, the largest contribution is made by the Amazon Basin. It shelters at least one thousand species and subspecies, grouped in seventy families. Nowhere else on earth has such a small group of ancestors differentiated into such a huge number of closely related species.

General Characteristics

In the Amazon forest, the easiest way to recognize species and genders of birds is by sight. Often, their calls play an important role in identification.

The Amazonian bird population is not necessarily made up of a great number of individuals. Unlike the temperate regions, only a few species are numerically dominant. On the contrary, each species in Amazonia is represented by relatively few individuals. For this reason, the forest can be disappointing to explorers at first sight.

Like all other forest dwellers, birds have adapted to living and moving in the thick vegetation. Some search for their food on the ground, perching on the lower horizons of vegetation in order to escape from ground predators. They have frail legs, but their toes and claws allow them to safely grasp branches. Some of them are completely incapable of moving on the ground and never land on it.

The wings of these birds, both birds of prey and other species, have varied, often rounded shapes. These shapes do not allow for the great acrobatic grace and speed that birds of open environments have developed. They are, however, more versatile. All these birds are capable of abrupt changes in direction and quick movements among trunks and branches.

Many Amazonian birds nest in tree trunks. Some dig their own holes. Others use natural cavities. Still others use nests constructed by birds better adapted for this work. Woodpeckers, barbets, parrots, trogons, and members of the family Dendrocolaptidae all nest in this manner.

Nonmigratory Birds

The majority of birds in the Amazon are not migratory, since the forest provides them with constantly favorable conditions. The availability of food is especially favorable. These conditions ensure that reproductive activity can occur throughout most of the year.

The blue macaw possesses a bright blue back with a yellow underside. It is found from Panama to Argentina. It makes its home on the riverbanks of the rain forest, in savannas with scattered trees and palms, and in the llanos. Like all other birds, the macaw is very hard to find in the Amazon forest. Birds hide themselves in the thick vegetation. In particular, the most colorful varieties never leave the treetops. In order to see them, one must wait patiently beside a blossoming or fruit-bearing tree or along a river. The birds can be seen as they descend from tall trees. Such a sight can be a truly unforgettable and marvelous experience.

However, birds do travel throughout the forest. When they are not nesting, they explore vast areas, searching for food that is not available everywhere. The vegetation in the different sections of forest does not grow in synchronized rhythms. Instead, the life cycle of each varies according to the orientation of the slopes, the microclimatic (uniform local climate of a small habitat) conditions, and soil characteristics. Ecological factors are only constant over vast regions. Birds, opportunists by nature, take advantage of the available food as best they can. In addition to seasonal movements that are tied to climatic fluctuations, birds also make daily flights. Some birds fly every day from their nests or from the places where they spend their nights, to their feeding grounds. Large parrots, in particular the macaws that can be seen crossing rivers in pairs or small groups, sometimes travel considerable distances in search of food. Small flocks made up of individuals of different species sometimes tour the forest during the day. Often they follow columns of ants, upon whom some species feed. Some birds take advantage of the confusion caused by the ants' passage to feed upon other insects and small vertebrates.

The organization of these strange groups can be explained as a kind of mutualism, because all of the birds benefit from the agitation caused by their passage. A certain behavioral affinity also comes into play. Otherwise such an alliance between fruit- and insect-eating species would be difficult to explain. These groups also provide a better defense against predators. Individuals of different species fly at varying levels of vegetation and are able to warn the others with cries of alarm if predators are near.

It is important to note that the Amazonian forests host some migratory species coming from unstable climatic zones. These include some birds of prey and some birds that feed upon airborne insects. In the forest, the quantity of food is constant throughout the year. There are no periods of surplus. This is the opposite of what happens in the savannas, where alternating periods of dryness and rain produce either an abundance or a shortage.

Land Species

The birds of the Amazon dwell within well-defined vegetational horizons. Some love the sunlight and always stay at treetop level. Others live in the lower layers of this three-dimensional universe. Still others inhabit the ground. Some large birds feed on the ground but, during the night,

The green toucan is immediately recognized by its enormous beak. The toucans are the most characteristic birds of the American tropics. There are thirty-seven species from southern Mexico to Argentina. They are true clowns, and it is very entertaining to observe them in groups. Their postures are as strange as their method of seizing their food, which consists of fruit, large insects, and, occasionally, small lizards. The toucan breaks fruit open by using the serrated edge of its beak. Then it throws a mouthful into the air and catches it in flight with its open beak.

perch on trees in order to escape predators. The most terrestrial birds in the forest are the tinamous, members of the family Tinamidae, which are primitive looking birds found only in South and Central America. Ornithologists place them in between the emu and the ostrich. They are well adapted to different environments, including the desert. In the Amazon are several species whose size varies between that of a quail and that of a rooster. Their plumage is brown, cream, and black. They resemble the shades of dead leaves and the bushes among which they move, looking for fruits, seeds, and large insects. When startled, tinamous fly clumsily for short distances and then sneak back into the bushes where they are camouflaged.

The mating habits of these birds represent a true reversal of sexual behavior. It is the female that attracts and courts the male with parades and flutelike calls. The male broods the eggs. These eggs are as shiny as porcelain with a greenish purple color. When the eggs hatch, the males take care of the young nestlings. They are covered with a creamy down with darker stripes and spots.

Some birds characteristic of very humid, forested zones are the trumpeters. They are in the genus *Psophia*, which is

The family Cracidae includes birds even smaller than the curassows, such as the guans. Their plumage varies from greenish gray to brown and are identical in both sexes. These species also feed in flocks, eating seeds and fruit, which they collect on the ground. They also hunt larvae and insects, scratching at the soil with their sturdy claws. The birds that belong to the Cracidae family are, however, decidedly more at ease in the trees than species belonging to the family Tinamidae. In fact, they are the only members of the order Galliformes that nest in the trees. The nest is built with twigs and holds two or three whitish eggs, which are large in comparison with the size of the bird. In the photograph is a female Spix's guan and its nestling.

made up of only three species, all found in the Amazon. These birds are placed by ornithologists between the rails and the cranes. They are about 18 inches (45 cm) long and have bulky bodies that rest on long legs. They are almost incapable of flying but can run swiftly on the ground and also swim skillfully. They are highly social birds, gathering in flocks numbering about one hundred. During their mating parades, they perform dances and leaps similar to those of cranes. Indians hunt them for their delicious meat and, as they are easily domesticated, also raise them with chickens. Their loud, sharp calls, which have earned them the name of "trumpeters," is a useful warning system when danger draws near.

Other terrestrial birds characteristic of the Amazon are the curassows, which are the size of a turkey but not as bulky. The head of the males is crowned by a crest of curly feathers that can be raised up and down. The beak is adorned by a bright yellow protuberance. The male's plumage is black with a white underside, while the female's is brown.

The soil level is also the habitat of some members of the order Passeriformes, among whom are those of the

The Brazilian scarlet tanager is a typical representative of a splendidly colored family of small passerines. The birds live in the thickest parts of the forests. South American birds are notable both for the extraordinary variety of species (3,500 species from Mexico to Patagonia) and for their remarkably even distribution on most of the continent.

genus *Conopophaga*. These small birds, approximately 6 inches (15 cm) in length, have thickset bodies with large heads and very short tails. Their plumage is blackish brown, at times spotted with white. As with all terrestrial birds, their strong, lengthy tarsi (bones of the upper foot) permit agile movements. This is especially useful for rummaging among dead leaves for insects and berries. Because of their sharp, whistling cries, they have been named *chupa-denta* ("those that suck their teeth") by the Brazilians. The ground is also the chosen environment for birds of the genera *Formicarius* and *Grallaria*, whose profiles, with their short tails and ungainly aspects, resemble those of *Conopophaga*. They also resemble Old World members of the genus *Pitta* and are, in fact, their ecological counterparts, lacking only their splendid coloration.

Many other birds of the genus *Formicarius* perch upon the ground. Some build their nests there, while others construct nesting on the lower vegetation levels. They attain varying, but always modest, sizes. Their plumage is brown, black, and white. They specialize in pillaging the columns of ants that march everywhere throughout the forest.

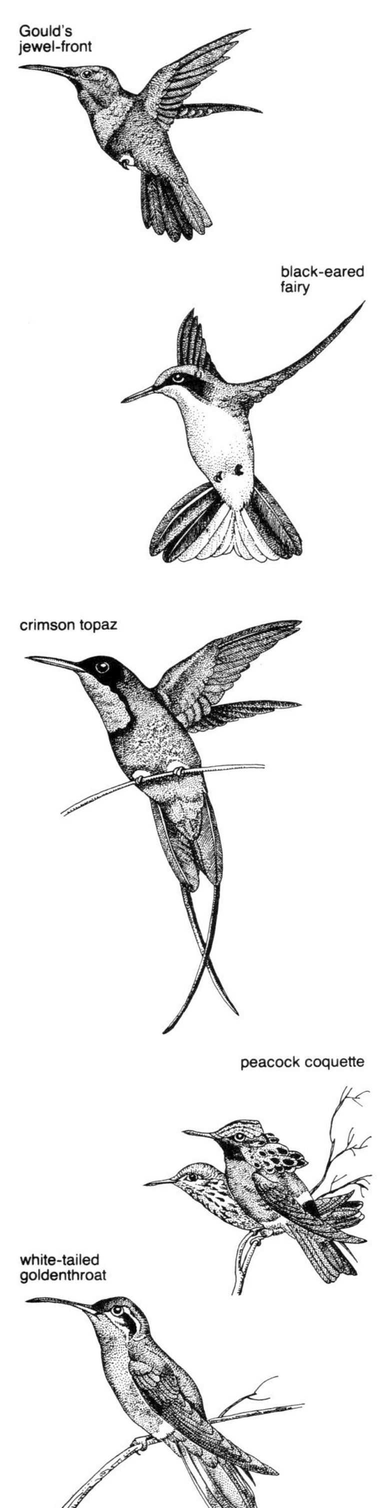

Species of Lower Vegetation Levels

Sometimes the lower vegetation level of the primary forest is absent. But it does exist in clearings alongside streams and wherever old plantations have been taken over by undergrowth. Many birds have found refuge in these clearings, especially those species that take sustenance from the riverbeds.

Most of these birds have faintly colored plumage that enables them to blend in with their environment and escape the eyes of predators. Some hummingbirds characteristic of the low vegetation are in the genus *Phaethornis* and family Trochilidae. Unlike their multicolored relatives, these birds have somber brown and gray plumage with stripes of black and white. They also have curved beaks. Even more so than their relatives, they must feed on insects because flowers rich in nectar are rare in the underbrush.

Hummingbirds are antisocial loners, intolerant when others of their kind draw near. *Phaethornis*, however, do not conform to this rule. To attract females, males gather in small flocks in the forest and perch on separate branches. They show off in a sort of choral competition despite the relative monotony of their songs. After having expressed himself, each male flies off to perform aerial tricks between the trees before returning to perch among his comrades. The nests of these birds are hidden among bushes and under fronds of ferns.

In shady areas of thick vegetation live the manakins of

Opposite page: Hummingbirds are the smallest birds in the world, weighing as little as 0.07 ounce. They have extraordinary flying skills. Their light, long wings vibrate at a rate of fifty to eighty beats per second, producing a hum that can be heard from a distance. The hummingbird's method of flight is unique and enables it to make sudden changes in direction or to stay suspended in midair. They can even fly backward. To power this extraordinarily precise mechanism, hummingbirds have short, powerful muscles. Their hearts are very large in relation to the size of their bodies.

Shown are some stages of the mating parade of the golden-headed manakin. Perched on a twig, the bird slides backward, beating its wings and bending its body into various postures. The manakins are acrobatic and can perform fantastic aerial maneuvers. That is why they are called *danadores* (by the Brazilians) and *bailadores* (by the Spanish-speaking people), words that mean "dancers." The manakins accompany their parades with calls that sound like the snapping of dry twigs, the croaks of frogs, and the rasp of thin metal sheets being shaken. The flapping of the wings and the noise of the wind rushing through their feathers add to this symphony.

the family Pipridae. Manakins do not exceed 4 inches (10 cm) in length and exhibit a marked sexual variation. The males are brightly colored with a plumage of green, red, yellow, and black with some iridescent feathers. The females have a more discrete coloration that ranges from green to yellow. Manakins feed on fruits and insects. The courting parades of these birds are collective and occur in the same areas of the forest year after year. Males gather in flocks of twenty and perch in full sight on low branches. These branches and the underlying ground have been stripped of all leaves. There is great confusion as the birds fly from branch to branch and engage in courting behaviors from their perches. At times, one of them will land and perform strange movements as if to display its colorful plumage. The females are attracted by these performances that vary from species to species, particularly as regards the aggressiveness of the males. In some species, the parades are truly collective. In others, each male claims its own territory, even if it is very close to that of its rivals. Sometimes, the females join the males in a dual dance and mate afterward on a nearby branch. For other species, the ritual is more complex. First, one male comes forward. Then, a second male follows and lands beside the first. The pair then performs a perfectly synchronized dance. They do this alone, at first, and then in the presence of the female. The female mates with only one of the two males and only after this dual performance. After mating, the males, who mate with more than one female, leave their companion and return to their perch. The females build their nests alone in the fork of two branches. They care for the offspring them-

About 1 foot (30 cm) long, the cock-of-the-rock is one of the most beautiful birds imaginable. The males have a silky, bright orange plumage, against which their black wings and white chests contrast sharply. Their heads are surrounded by crests of feathers forming a disclike structure. Their bright plumage seems to capture the light that penetrates the dim underbrush.

selves. A similar behavior characterizes the cock-of-the-rock, belonging to the family Cotingidae. These birds usually live in the heart of the thick forest, close to rocky outcrops and rivers. They love to bathe several times a day. Their mating parade is also very unusual and complex. The males gather in small groups in areas of the forest that they have swept clean of leaves. There, they perform their parades, engaging in acrobatic dances. They flutter their wings and tails as if to show off their spectacular plumage. The females, with brown plumage, are attracted by these parades. After mating briefly, they will build their nests in rocky holes. The nests are made of mud, reinforced with twigs and covered with mosses and lichens. The females of this species care for their nestlings alone.

Species of the Trunks and Branches

Some birds are not easy to place within a particular horizon of the forest because they move up and down along the tree trunks. In this group are found the woodpeckers. They have differentiated into a great number of species in the Amazon region. Some woodpeckers have colorations resembling cork, while others are brightly colored. They

Two of the many Amazonian species of cuckoos are pictured. Their long tapered tails help them move easily through the thick canopy of the trees. They hop from branch to branch almost like a squirrel.

probe the trunks for insects, poking holes in the wood with their sturdy beaks.

The habits of the woodpeckers are shared by the species *Dendrocolaptes* belonging to the family Dendrocolaptidae. These birds are unique to the Americas, and in the Amazon forest they are represented by a large number of species. They vary from 6 to 14 inches (15 to 35 cm) in length. They resemble the short-toed tree creepers of the family Certidae, but they are not related. This is an example of evolutionary convergence involving a similarity of habits. The feet have elongated toes, and the tail is equipped with pointed rectrices (tail feathers that help control flight direction) similar to those of a woodpecker. These adaptations enable them to keep a firm grip on branches and move swiftly up and down trunks. The beak can be straight or hooked, but it is always narrow. These birds are able to catch insects and larvae hidden under the cork of trees or within epiphytic plants. They cannot, however, poke holes in wood the way the woodpecker does. Their plumage has brown, cream, and black tints, making an ideal camouflage against the cork.

dark-billed cuckoo

pavaninus cuckoo

Species of the Suspended Environment

Many birds found in the trees belong to various families. The Columbidae, seed-eaters, are rare because there is not enough food in this environment for them. Fruit-eaters, on the other hand, are highly diversified. They include the parrots, of which there are about thirty species. The Amazon is one of the most important areas of diversification for these birds.The largest parrots are the macaws and are present in numerous species. They have a brightly colored plumage and a long tail that makes them easy to recognize in flight. The Amazon parrots, less elegant in form, have shorter tails. They can be recognized by the color of their heads, which are a mix of red, blue, and yellow tints.

Amazon parrots are often raised in captivity by Indians. The native populations sometimes even increase the variety of color in the parrots' head feathers through skilled manipulations. These Indians pluck the feathers from the birds' heads and rub their skins with liquids extracted from different species of frogs. The new feathers absorb the pigments contained in these liquids and take on unusual colorations. The first explorers were surprised and puzzled when they encountered these artificially colored birds.

Several species of cuckoos also live in the Amazon.

After mating, the male hummingbird leaves the female. The female builds its nest, made of moss, twigs, and lichens. The nest is usually hidden among the leaves, and it is strengthened underneath by cobwebs (as the nest of *Glaucis hirsuta* in the picture shows.) The female lays two eggs which she will tend for about a month. The young birds leave the nest after they learn to fly.

Unlike their relatives in colder climates, they do not exploit other birds but build their own nests and raise their own nestlings.

Hummingbirds are also typical of the upper layer of vegetation. It is hard to imagine more splendid creatures than these birds, especially the males with their multi-colored plumage.

All ninety hummingbird species living in Amazonia feed on highly nutritious substances, such as the nectar of flowers. They gather in groups around blossoming plants, in spite of their combative and individualistic natures. They hover in front of blossoms, wagging their long, narrow, extensible tongues that function like medicine droppers. They suck in nectar, a sugary substance contained in the flowers, then fly to another flower cluster or stop to rest.

These tiny birds also feed on insects that they seize from flowers, leaves, or branches. Some species, like the flycatcher, catch insects in flight. They may also steal insects trapped in cobwebs and even prey on a spider if it is sufficiently small.

The males hover near their food sources, each covering a small territory. They violently chase away intruders with sharp trills. Males attract females into their territories by performing aerial acrobatics when they see them close by. They execute an actual dance, flying in circles, gliding, and showing off their splendid, glittering plumage. The female, almost invariably less colorful than the male, eventually joins in the acrobatics. They engage in a dual dance during which mating often occurs.

In the forest, sheltered by the intricate vegetation, live the trogons. Medium-sized, around 12 inches (30 cm) long, the males have extravagant plumage. They have golden green backs and bright yellow or red undersides. These animals usually remain in the shade, which makes them very difficult to spot. It is possible to see them when they race from their perches to catch an insect in flight or to pick a piece of fruit. They nest in holes that they excavate in rotting trunks or logs of wood soft enough for their rather delicate beaks. Some may even use the paper nests of wasps after devouring the insects and their larvae.

Just below this suspended environment lives a group of very shy birds, the Bucconidae. The Brazilians call them *Juan Bobos* because, to them, the birds seem lazy. The Bucconidae are short, with large heads and a rather dull plumage. This is in sharp contrast with the features of their

closest relatives, the jacamars of the family Galbulidae. These are birds with long, sharp beaks and intense green or metallic blue plumage. The jacamars live at the edges of clearings or on open ground. They skillfully hunt insects, especially large butterflies.

Many other birds, each more incredible than the next, are found in the treetops. First and foremost are the toucans, belonging to the family Ramphastidae. These are easily recognized by their huge bill, which in some species is almost as long as the entire body. It is always intensely colored. The barbets are placed in the same order as the toucans (Piciformes) and belong to the family Capitonidae. The Amazon hosts six species, all medium-sized bulky birds that owe their name to the presence of whiskers which jut from the sides of their beaks. Birds with brightly colored plumage and lively, restless natures, they roam the trees looking for insects, buds, and fruit.

Birds belonging to the family Cotingidae are highly varied, ranging in size from that of a starling to that of a crow. Some have a pure white plumage, such as the white bellbird. This bird certainly cannot camouflage itself in the thick vegetation. Others are intensely colored, with glossy black, blue, purple or red feathers. Among the most beautiful is the Pompadour cotinga with a superb, deep violet plumage. This bird was named for the famous Marquise de Pompadour by a gallant British ornithologist who had obtained the first specimen from the cargo of a captured French ship.

The ornamentations of the birds of this group are widely diversified. The parasol bird is the size of a crow and has a glossy blue plumage. On its head, is a "parasol" of feathers that can be raised up and down and is the feature that earned it its name. A feathered protuberance about 12 inches (30 cm) long hangs from its throat. These ornaments are prominently displayed during the mating parades. Some of these birds are mute, while others emit powerful calls. An example of the latter is the white bellbird, so called because its song recalls the sound of a carillon and echoes throughout the forest.

Many other birds living in the forests deserve mention. The major families include the American flycatcher, which has several species. Some live in the underbrush and others among the treetops. All are insect eaters. The same is true of the vireos, small birds with a greenish or yellowish plumage, and of the tanagers, which belong to the family Thrau-

vireo Tangara

paradise tanager

pidae. The latter are especially common in the Amazon. Tanagers are colorful dwellers of the thickest parts of the forest. They feed on tender shoots, fruits, and insects. Although not as splendid as the hummingbirds, they are nevertheless regarded as jewels of the Amazon forest. There are other areas to investigate: the edges of the forests, the clearings, and the campsites of Indians and explorers. These places attract the most species of birds outside the dense forest. Numerous flycatchers hunt in the open air, and flocks of small seed-eaters raid the fields. There are also some extraordinary birds belonging to the family Icteridae. They can be as long as 16 inches (40 cm). Often they perch on treetops and survey their territory, sounding the alarm if birds of prey draw near. These flocks of birds, always very busy, enliven campsites much as the weaverbirds do in Africa.

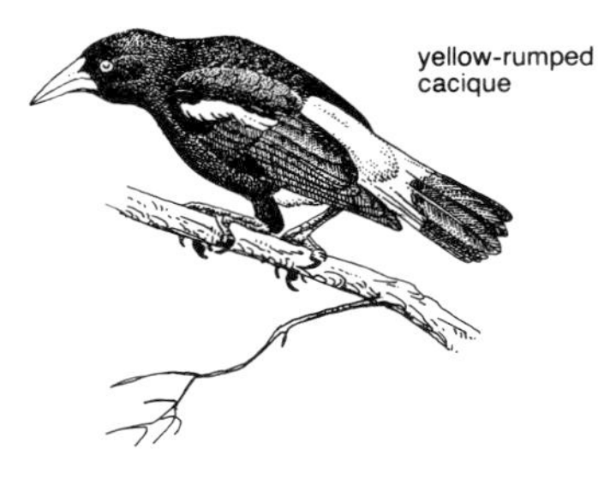

yellow-rumped cacique

Feeding Options

Birds in the Amazon forest occupy different ecological niches. They take advantage of all the possibilities offered by their particular environment and develop varied feeding habits.

The great availability and variety of fruit throughout the year explains the presence of large numbers of fruit-eating birds. Sometimes the fruit supply is overly plentiful, but there are never periods of serious scarcity. Fruit is a dependable and highly nutritious food source that plays a major role in the ecosystems of the tropical forests with hot and humid climates. In the Amazon as well as in Guyana, great numbers of birds rely upon this bountiful resource.

troupial Crax

The fruit-eaters are found in all layers of the forest vegetation. At the lowest level, the curassows peck at fallen fruits. At the highest layer, parrots, tanagers, and other birds take fruit directly from the trees. At this point, it is important to speak about the relationships that exist between birds and fruit-eating mammals (bats, marsupials, and rodents), and the plants that provide them with their food. In one sense, these animals have a negative impact upon the trees because they consume their fruit. But they also help in spreading their seeds. Mammals are attracted by the color and smell of ripe fruit and, therefore, eat large quantities. Afterward, they expel the seeds with their droppings, spreading them throughout the forest. Recent studies have proven that this mechanism is of primary importance to the process of reforestation.

black curassow

In the Amazon forests, various birds of prey live along the rivers, where they can take advantage of the open spaces to catch frogs, reptiles, birds, and insects. Two of these birds of prey are the yellow-throated caracara (which also eats palm fruits) and the black-faced hawk (which usually preys on the birds that follow armies of ants).

Flower nectar also plays a major role as food for some specialized birds, especially the hummingbirds. This precious liquid, supplemented by insects in the diet, is the main food source in these warm regions. Other birds share this diet, earning them the name of "sugarbirds" (members of the family Coerebidae). These are small birds with an intensely colored plumage and sharp, narrow beaks that are inserted into flowers. These birds perform the important task of pollinating flowers. While they are sucking in the nectar, some pollen gets stuck to their feathers. Eventually, they will leave some of this pollen on other flowers, ensuring the cross-pollination that is crucial to plants' survival. Some nectar-eating bats perform the same operation on flowers that open only during the night. These relationships are clearly advantageous to both plant and animal.

The second major food resource in the Amazon is insects. Their great numbers and diversity have already been mentioned. They can be eaten by both random as well as highly specialized predators. Each bird chooses a hunting technique and, accordingly, seeks a specific kind of prey. This differentiation can be observed even within different species of the same family. Flycatchers are an excellent example. Some of them hunt on the ground. Others, such as the leaf warblers and the blackcaps, scan the treetops. Many groups of birds hide and wait for their prey in the different layers of the forest. They perch on a branch, surveying their surroundings, ready to swoop on insects that are the right size. The larger insect-eaters exhibit behavior like that of the shrike. They not only seize large insects, killing them with their sturdy, hooked beaks, but also (like true birds of prey) attack even reptiles and small birds. It is important to remember that besides birds with extremely specialized eating habits, the forest also shelters many species with highly varied diets.

yellow-throated caracara

The birds of prey are the last group of birds to be discussed. Predators are attracted in large numbers by the availability of prey, such as reptiles, birds, and mammals. Besides owls, which are nocturnal birds of prey, many daylight predators can be found. These include buzzards, sparrow hawks, and falcons, which perch in the trees until they swoop down on their prey with a swift plunge. The bat falcon preys upon birds, even on the fastest species, such as swifts, swallows and hummingbirds. It also hunts bats.

black-faced hawk

Much larger birds of prey, such as the Guyana crested eagle, also dwell in the Amazon. This bird can weigh up to

The turkey vulture and the king vulture *(pictured here)* feed on dead fish, carrion, and garbage. They find food with their sense of smell. Usually the sense of smell is poor in birds. The vulture's peculiar feature might explain their presence in an enclosed environment such as the Amazonian forest, where eyesight alone is not very useful. Relatives of these vultures in Africa and Asia have no sense of smell and thus cannot hunt in the woods and are not found in tropical forests.

4.5 pounds (2 kg) and has a small crest on its head. It hunts small monkeys, opossums, birds, and lizards. It is surpassed in size by the gigantic harpy eagle, the largest bird of prey in the world. This majestic bird, weighing up to 11 pounds (5 kg), is distinguished by its blackish blue back and white belly. It has an enormous head adorned by a crest composed of two uplifted feathers. Its beak is as dangerous as its enormous claws. In spite of its size, it is difficult to spot because it rarely flies over the forest. It usually prefers to move beneath the tree covering in order to surprise its prey. It hunts all of the large animals of the forest, including opossums, coatis, and porcupines. It particularly likes monkeys and sloths.

Included among the forest birds of prey is the vulture. Some species live along the rivers where they seize their share of carrion (dead animals). The most highly specialized species, are American vultures. The black vulture is rarely found in the heart of the forest, preferring to follow the movements of people. It is often seen in large cities, where it is a scavenger. The turkey vulture and the king vulture, both forest species, have light plumage and featherless heads and necks covered with bright yellow skin.

MAMMALS

In accordance with developments in the geological history of the continent, mammals of South American origin have undergone an unusual evolutionary process. Some groups belonging to this class of vertebrates have never succeeded in penetrating this part of the world because of its long geographical isolation. This isolation has come to an end in relatively recent time with the formation of Central America. Entire groups, elsewhere well developed, are here either completely absent or of only minor importance in the biology of the community. Those groups that managed to spread into South America when it was still connected with other continents have evolved in their own way. Often they have undergone profound transformations. In some cases, large numbers of species have rapidly diversified from shared ancestors. Each one of these species has highly specialized adaptations. Species belonging to the genus *Macrauchenia* are a good example of this process. Apart from birds, mammals are among the best represented groups of vertebrates in the Amazon forest.

Mammals of the Land

Land, water, and their interconnectedness are the dominating facts of life in Amazonia. This fact explains why many of the animals that inhabit Amazonia have developed adaptations for both types of habitats. Species belonging to the family Cervidae (hoofed mammals) are a good example of this dual adaptation. The white-tailed deer is one of the most extraordinarily flexible species found throughout America from Canada to Peru. It can be found in the northernmost forests of America as well as in the subdesert regions and in the heart of Amazonia.

Another kind of deer, the brocket deer, is found in the Amazon region in the form of two species *(Mazama americana* and *M. gouazoubira).* These animals do not exceed 27.5 inches (70 cm) at the shoulder and can weigh about 45 pounds (20 kg). Their simple horns, which do not branch, are about 5 inches (12 cm) long. Like most of the forest deer, these animals are solitary and form pairs only during the mating period. Like the white-tailed deer, the brocket deer has a diet of leaves and tender shoots. They are extremely vulnerable to predators. To escape attack, they will not hesitate to jump into water or to wade across large rivers. Observing these small deer, it can be seen that they are South America's ecological counterparts to the large African duikers (antelope), such as the light-backed duiker.

Opposite: A sloth climbs its favorite tree, the Cecropia, to feed on the tender leaves which constitute most of its diet. These animals deserve their name. For one thing, they spend most of their time sleeping. Even when they are awake, they are almost motionless. When they do move, they do so extremely slowly.

These drawings illustrate the amazing evolutionary convergence which exists among some large Amazonian rodents and some small African hoofed mammals. From left to right are the paca and the African water chevrotain *(top row)* and the agouti and the pygmy antelope *(bottom row)*. These animals are ecological counterparts. Although they belong to different classifications, they occupy similar ecological niches on each side of the Atlantic Ocean. It is almost as if nature has repeated itself—creating, with different elements, the same community of animals that occupies the same niches and that uses the same food resources.

These two groups of deer, belonging to different families, have the same body shape and similar horns. This is an obvious example of evolutionary convergence caused by adaptation to similar yet separate environmental conditions and habitats. It has been established that the deer of South America have not further diversified to provide counterparts to the small African duikers. These niches have been taken over by rodents, the agoutis. These graceful animals can weigh up to 9 pounds (4 kg), which is light for a hoofed mammal but quite heavy for a rodent. The resemblance between agoutis and duikers is surprising. Both have the same head shape, thin legs, a short tail, and similar behavior. The nails of the agoutis are almost transformed into hoofs. Moreover, agoutis have short, rough, reddish brown fur, resembling that of small antelope. Both duikers and agoutis occupy the same ecological niche and are perfectly adapted to move in the thickest vegetation due to their small size and narrow, elongated shape. They feed on tender leaves and shoots as well as fruit that has fallen to the ground. The behavioral and social patterns of these two animals are also similar. Both are solitary or live in small groups in the forest or along the riverbanks.

white-lipped peccary

collared peccary

The white-lipped peccary and the collared peccary are eagerly sought by the Indians.The meat of these animals is a major food source.

A similar adaptive convergence can be observed by comparing the African and Asian musk deer with another group of South American rodents, the pacas. These two groups of animals are similar in size and have the same spotted fur. They also live in the same habitats, which are thick forests close to rivers or swamps. Even their movements and behavior are surprisingly alike.

The most typical hoofed mammals of the region are the peccaries, counterparts of the European boars. There are two different species, the collared peccary and the white-lipped peccary. The first is smaller and may be found as far north as Arizona. This fact suggests it has a remarkable capacity for adaptation. Although sharing the same habitat, these two species do not enter into competition. Both live in groups. The collared peccary is established in groups of about fifteen. The white-lipped peccary roams in groups of nearly one hundred. Peccaries travel through forests, looking for roots, bulbs, and fallen fruit that they detect with their very fine sense of smell. They may also feed on meat, either carrion or larvae, that they find on the forest floor. Their sense of hearing is acute, but their eyesight is weak.

One very unusual animal is the Brazilian tapir, whose appearance startled the first explorers. The size of a pony, it has a rudimentary (imperfectly developed) tail and a sort of elongated, fleshy snout. It has hooves, and for this reason it is considered closely related to horses. This is a true living fossil whose only close relatives inhabit tropical Asia.

The Brazilian tapir prefers swampy habitats and areas along the riverbanks. There it wanders, looking for fruit, leaves, rhizomes, and roots. It keeps to its territory, within which it creates and regularly uses its own trails. It leads a solitary life or stays within a small family group. The female gives birth to one baby each year. The fur of the young is spotted, which helps hide it from predators. Tapirs are shy, as are all forest animals. Moreover, they are nocturnal animals, active mainly at night. Thus, they can be observed only after long and patient waiting.

Another ground dweller of the forest is the giant anteater, a creature that seems to have survived from ancient times. It is a little over 4 feet (1.3 m) long with a bushy tail 2.4 feet (75 cm) long. It can weigh up to 50 pounds (23 kg). its body is elongated and laterally flattened. The head is largish and tapered. It has a tubular, tiny mouth through which its sticky tongue moves in and out.

The three-toed anteater leads a solitary life except during mating periods, when it lives in pairs for a short time. This animal is common outside the Amazon. Its range extends to the plains of northern Argentina.

This is the organ with which the anteater traps the ants and termites that form its diet. It destroys ant and termite nests with its strong paws armed with hooked claws. The claws are so huge that they cause the anteater to move with a peculiar gait. It walks on its knuckles with its claws bent backward. Giant anteaters were once placed in the order Edentata along with armadillos, but, in fact, these two animals are not related. Armadillos are typical of the Americas and thrive in every type of environment. They prefer the open ground but have also managed to occupy the forests.

They are recognized by the shapes of their bodies and by their armorlike carapaces. These are composed of horny plates that overlap across the animal's back. The head is also covered by a similar shield made of the same substance. Armadillos can move quite swiftly but usually defend themselves by curling up in a ball that is invulnerable to predators. Their paws have sturdy claws that enable them to dig deep burrows in the ground. They spend most of their day in these shelters. Their claws are also useful for raking the ground in search of ants and termites, which form most of their diet.

Armadillos are an extremely specialized group of mammals. Their shape and physiology have some special features that are not found in any other animal of their class. The females, for example, give birth to numerous offspring. Sometimes there are as many as a dozen, all generated from a single egg. This means all of the offspring are identical genetically, a rare occurrence among most mammals.

Some Tree-Dwelling Mammals

Tree-dwelling mammals are more numerous than terrestrial varieties. One species related to the giant anteater, the colored anteater, or tamandua, is well adapted to its arboreal habitat. Its small size and sturdy nails allow supple movements among branches and up and down trunks. A close relative, the silky or two-toed anteater, is more nocturnal. It has softer fur, a shorter snout, and a prehensile tail. Both species feed on ants and termites, which they catch after having disrupted the nests with their claws.

Other tree mammals are mainly vegetarian, even though some may supplement their diets with food of animal origin. Among the rodents are the rice rat, the spiny rat, and one porcupine, the prehensile-tailed porcupine, or coendou. The coendou possesses a long, prehensile tail that functions as its fifth limb. The kinkajou, a carnivore, has a short snout and a long prehensile tail like that of the coendou. Marsupials include the opossums. They are rather primitive mammals, for which America and Australia represent the last shelter. The same habitat may sustain as many as five or six different species of opossums belonging to various genera (*Didelphis, Philander, Marmosa, Caluromys*).

Although all of these species consume the same plants, each one has specialized so as to keep competition at a minimum and best distribute the available food. Some tree

Pictured are three typical mammals of the Amazonian forest: the kinkajou (a carnivore), the murine opossum, and the gray four-eyed opossum. The opossums are marsupials.

mammals, for example, have specialized in eating seeds, although they do not totally avoid fruit. This is true of small rodents that can attack the tough exterior of fruit with their strong teeth and reach inside for seeds. The coendou, weighing up to 11 pounds (5 kg) and thus relatively big, gathers large, tough fruit and opens them to extract large quantities of seeds. Other tree mammals are mostly fruit-eaters, choosing to feed on the fruit pulp. The marsupials supplement their fruit diet with some animal prey.

Various species can also be divided according to which horizon of the forest they inhabit. This is especially true of the opossums. On the lowest horizon of vegetation, three different opossums are found. They vary significantly in size so as not to enter into competition with each other to any great extent. The smallest species is the Murine opossum, weighing about 1.7 ounces (50 g). It spends most of its time among the upper branches but does come down to the ground. The gray "four-eyed" opossum, named for the two characteristic white spots on its forehead, weighs about 14 ounces (400 g). It searches for its food on the ground, eating insects, earthworms, occasional carrion, and fruit that has fallen from the trees. Lastly, the North American opossum, has been called *pian* (related to a French word that means "smelly") in Guyana because of its bad odor. It weighs up to 2.2 pounds (1 kg). This animal can hunt on the ground, but it often climbs trees. Its diet is composed mainly of fruit, especially the larger varieties that are not eaten by smaller species. It also supplements its diet with worms and insects.

Other marsupials, in contrast, keep to the tree foliage. Another type of Murine opossum, the tiny *Marmosa cinerea*, weighs about 2.8 ounces (80 g). It captures tiny prey that can escape other, less swift opossums. It also consumes many fruits. The woolly opossum, much larger at 10.5 ounces (300 g), is almost exclusively a fruit-eater.

All of these examples, taken from a recent study conducted in French Guyana, prove that it is possible to find a community of animals living within the same habitat that rely upon the same food resources.

kinkajou

murine opossum

gray four-eyed opossum

Sloths

The most strictly arboreal mammals living in the Amazon are the sloths. These animals were once placed in the order Edentata, despite the fact that they have teeth. In South America, two genera differ in the number of toes their members have. These are the three-toed sloths (*Bradypus*

The coendou, or prehensile-tailed porcupine, is a tree-dweller. This spiny rodent, which has spread all the way to North America, has a long prehensile tail and is an exceptional climber.

tridactylus and related species) and the two-toed sloths (*Choloepus hoffmanni* and its relatives). These two genera are biologically very similar. A sloth vaguely resembles a small teddy bear with its rounded shape, globelike head, long limbs, and the thick bristly fur that covers its body. The color of its fur varies from brown to gray but often has a greenish tint. This is produced by microscopic algae that develop on the surface of the hair and thrive due to the warm, humid climate of the forest. Moreover, the larvae of a butterfly live in symbiosis with these algae. These larvae are so at ease on the sloth's fur that they will eventually fly away as adult butterflies and deposit their eggs on yet another sloth.

Despite their desire to sleep a great deal and the slow manner in which they move about, sloths are extraordinarily strong. They have extremely sturdy claws, which enable them to cling firmly to branches while hanging upside down. In this position they sleep or wander about, seeking their favorite trees belonging to the genus *Cecropia*. The leaves of such trees are their main, if not their only, food source. After filling themselves, they digest their meal in a

The squirrel monkey is a typical, small South American monkey. Members of the family Callithricidae, generally called "marmosets," are even smaller than the squirrel monkey. Some marmoset species are on the verge of extinction as a result of the destruction of the forest.

peculiar digestive organ divided into several chambers. The first chamber has very muscular walls and is used to crush the leaves mechanically. In the succeeding chambers, chemical breakdown occurs. All in all, the sloth's stomach accounts for almost one-third of its weight. Once plant matter has been digested, the sloths descend to the ground to defecate at the base of trees. This usually happens once a week though sometimes more often. Then they slowly climb back into the tree tops, cling to a branch upside down, and sleep. Sloths are typical inhabitants of Amazonia, and their numbers are often high. But they go unnoticed, hidden by the vegetation. In order to spot them, the tops of trees beside riverbanks, often barren of leaves, must be watched carefully. These sloths are cautious and having wandered out of their usual camouflaged territory, they risk falling victim to harpy eagles.

Monkeys

In Amazonia, monkeys have diversified to an astounding degree. All American monkeys are placed within a special group and are referred to as platyrrhine monkeys. They have widely separated nostrils, giving their snout a very peculiar appearance, and an additional premolar tooth that monkeys of the Old World do not possess. All monkeys are thought to have developed from common ancestors and to have evolved independently on both sides of the Atlantic Ocean.

Monkeys are some of the most attractive animals of the Amazon. They are easily observed tree dwellers, active throughout the day, and extraordinarily lively. Some are tiny. The most minute is the pygmy marmoset, no longer than 6 inches (15 cm) not counting its long tail. It weighs about 2.5 ounces (70 g). Others belonging to the short-tusked marmoset group are between 7 and 11 inches (18 and 30 cm) long, excluding their tails. They weigh between 7 and 16 ounces (200 and 450 g). They have soft fur, a crown of hairy tufts on their ears, and "sideburns" of a color different from the rest of their fur.

All of these small monkeys, which have acute senses, live among trees and bushes in groups that are thought to be joined families. They communicate through mimicry and, mainly, through very loud and frequent cries. These have been compared to bird calls. During the day, they are very active and always searching for food. They eat insects, spiders, larvae, and bird eggs, as well as fruit and tender shoots of other plants. At night they find shelter in hollow trunks and in the forks of large branches. They are extremely sociable and quite intelligent but retain some primitive features. These include claws on all but their big toes, unlike the nails found in all other monkey species.

The squirrel monkey is larger in size, weighing from 1.6 to 2.4 pounds (750 to 1,100 g). Its fur is yellowish on the back and light hazel on the underside. Its white face and black snout are in contrast to the rest of the body.

Contrasted with these "elves" of the forest are the larger monkeys. The capuchins are represented by several species that can be distinguished from each other by the presence or absence of ear tufts.

The ukaris are much larger but have relatively short tails. Their rough fur gives them a disheveled look. The fur is dark brown in contrast with the color of their foreheads and faces, which are almost hairless and usually red or reddish

red-faced ukari

red-backed saki

woolly monkey

spider monkey

orange. The sakis, on the other hand, have heads covered in thick fur. This is especially true for red-backed sakis, which appear to have thick beards and wigs that fall down over their eyes into bangs. They also have thick, bushy tails. The woolly monkeys, resembling teddy bears, also have very bushy, prehensile tails. These animals are especially fond of hard-shelled nuts, which they easily crush in their powerful jaws. Their oddly prominent belly has earned them the local name *barrigudos*, meaning "pot belly."

Spider monkeys, with their frail bodies and extremely long limbs, give quite a different appearance. They vaguely resemble gibbons, but, unlike gibbons, they have long, prehensile tails. This animal is a real acrobat, able to swing from branch to branch, hanging from only one limb or by its tail. The spider monkey can grasp an object the size of a hazelnut and carry it to its mouth with its tail. The tail is equipped with sensory buds on the tip.

Another group of monkeys that cannot go unmentioned includes howler monkeys. These are surely the largest of the American monkeys, weighing between 15 and 20 pounds (7 and 9 kg). Their thick fur has, in most cases, a characteristic reddish brown color. They live in clans ranging from five to forty individuals. They defend their territory in the forest under the leadership of one or two dominant males. They have a large number of calls. In the mornings and evenings, their cries echo throughout the forest and can be heard as far as 2 miles (3 km) away. The loudness of these cries has earned them their name.

All monkeys are active during the day. At night they seek shelter in the trees. However, there is one species that is active mainly at night, the douroucouli, or night monkey. This animal is quite small, no longer than 14 inches (35 cm) excluding its tail. It weighs about 1.3 to 2.1 pounds (600 to 1,000 g). It has woolly grayish fur and a rounded head with very short ears. Two white patches above its eyes are separated by a black stripe on its forehead and bordered by two other black bands at its temples. This monkey spends the day inside a tree hole or within the thickest vegetation. It leaves its shelter only at night. Then it vents its great energy, through swift leaps and movements among the branches. Its eyesight in the darkness is excellent, as its very large eyes will attest. These eyes have earned it the peculiar name of "owl-monkey." Its vocalizations are very complex and loud, enabling it to communicate from afar with its kin. All of the monkeys are generally tree dwellers, and only some will

The howler monkey belongs to the six species that are found from Mexico to Argentina. They are especially numerous in the Amazon Basin. These are the largest monkeys of the Americas. This monkey has long fur, sometimes a bare face, and a prehensile tail.

descend to the ground from time to time. They gather in groups, more or less numerous according to species and circumstances. Their diet, mainly vegetarian, includes fruit, tender shoots, and buds. They also eat insects, spiders, larvae, and some small vertebrates, such as reptiles, birds, and bird eggs.

Most of the monkeys share the same environment and the same food resources. However, each species has developed special preferences that serve to lessen competition. Although they are mainly fruit-eaters, some will supplement their diet with varying quantities of animal proteins. The howler monkeys are essentially leaf eaters, and their digestive apparatus is capable of storing huge quantities of leaves. Since the leaves are not very nutritious, they must be eaten in very large amounts.

The size of the monkeys is another important factor in the diversification of their food choices. The smallest species must content themselves with fruit or prey that is proportionate to their size.

Last of all, is the night monkey. It captures nocturnal insects and is certainly the only monkey able to prey upon bats.

Bats

Bats abound in Amazonia. Some seek shelter in caves, but the thick tree cover offers even better possibilities. Especially suitable are tree holes, which the bats share with other very different animals. These include insects, lizards, centipedes and millipedes, snakes, and small mammals. Some bats simply hang upside down from branches. Others take advantage of the shapes of leaves or leaf clusters, which form a kind of tent that shelters them from the sun.

Bats are divided into numerous families comprising at least ninety species. Some are related to the bats of temperate regions, such as mouse-eared bats belonging to the genus *Myotis*. Most, however, belong to the large family Phyllostomatidae, found only in the tropical American region. The name of this family refers to their *nose leaves* (leafy extensions that surround the nostrils). The shape and size of these vary with different species. Together with the often unique ears, these appendages give bats an unreal and almost monsterlike appearance. Nose leaves and ears undoubtedly play a major role in helping these mammals orient themselves in their night flights by enabling them to recognize obstacles and prey.

This species of bat is called the "fringed-lipped bat." It fishes for its food. It seizes small fish that swim near the water surface with its claws. In Amazonia, as in many other tropical regions, bats eat fruit, nectar, fish, and meat, in addition to insects. The blood-eating, or vampire, bat is peculiar to Central and South America. It feeds only on the blood of living vertebrates.

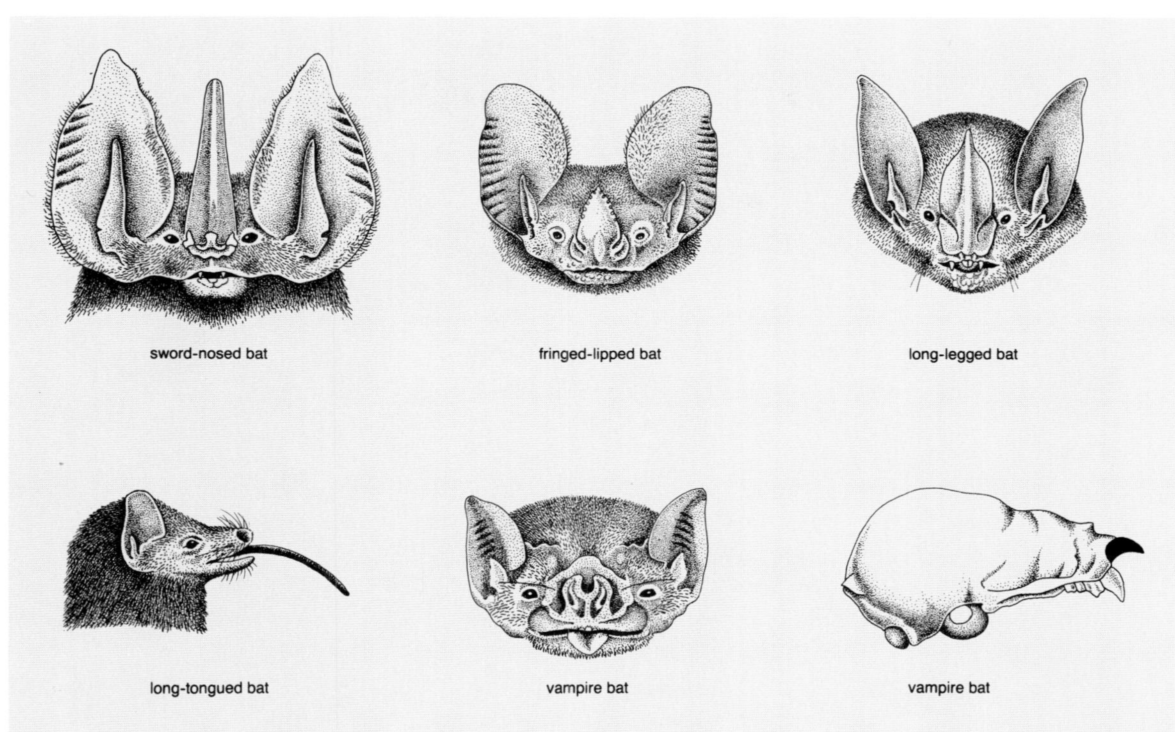

The three bats in the top row of the drawing belong to the family Phyllostomatidae, which are very common in tropical America. Members of this family all have strangely shaped nasal appendages. These "nose leaves" probably have something to do with directing the sound waves that reach the bats' extremely large ears. In the bottom row are *(left to right)* the long-tongued bat and the face and skull of the vampire bat, which belongs to the family Desmodontidae. The long-tongued bat is a nectar eater and a pollinator. The vampire bat also has nasal appendages. It is a ferocious blood-eater. It feeds on the blood of mammals, including humans.

Following page: The coatis use their long, ringed tails to help them balance while walking on the ground. Then they swiftly climb up vines and move among the trees.

It is well known that bats possess sonar devices that emit ultrasonic waves. These waves are deflected by any objects they find in their way. The echoes produced by deflected waves are perceived by the bats and guide them in their nighttime navigation.

As in all other regions of the world, bats in Amazonia awaken at dusk and fly in an uninterrupted dance until dawn. Persons walking on a trail through the forest will find themselves surrounded by these flying mammals. They will be brushed by the bat's wings and surely awed by the shrill shrieks the bats give out along with the ultrasonic transmissions.

All European bats are insect-eaters, and many species living in Amazonia share this diet. Some, however, have considerably enlarged the range of food upon which they depend. Some bats are fruit-eaters, swooping down in swarms upon fruit-laden trees to gorge themselves on the sugary, juicy pulp. Others, the long-nosed and long-tongued bats, are nectar-eaters. With their long, narrow tongues, they suck huge quantities of nectar from flowers which blossom only at night.

Still other species possess an even more specialized feeding pattern. The fisherman bat, also called the bulldog bat because of the shape of its head, has long, sharp claws.

It flies over the rivers and swiftly seizes small fish that swim near the surface. Other species are carnivores and hunt small rodents. The vampire bats, which are small despite human legend, feed only on blood. With their razor-sharp incisors, they easily cut through the skin of large mammals and cattle. A single vampire bat can suck up to 2 ounces (60 milliliters) of blood in one night. The number of bats is large, and sometimes they gather in flocks of several hundred. Their attacks may transmit rabies. Horses and cattle, however, are continuously exposed to attacks, which poses a serious economic and health problem.

The Predators

The large number of birds and mammals in the Amazon could not fail to attract predators. In the cat family (Felidae), there are tree dwellers, such as the little spotted cat and the ocelot. Both have thick, spotted coats. The jaguarundi is another tree dweller, whose fur is brownish gray. The family Mustelidae (including weasels and martens) is represented by numerous species. The most common is the tayra, weighing about 9 pounds (4 kg). It has brown fur although the head is somewhat lighter, and there is a white or yellow patch on its chest. The tayra moves swiftly on the ground and in the trees as well as being a good swimmer.

The largest cats, however, are all terrestrial animals. The puma, which has a uniform brown coat, lives mainly in the thick underbrush, usually not far from water. There, it stalks various prey, including some aquatic animals. The jaguar is the largest American cat. It has a reddish coat with black spots, a pattern similar to that of the leopard. Unlike the leopard, however, the jaguar has a large muzzle, likes the water, and is a fine swimmer. It rarely climbs trees, as it is seriously hindered in this activity by its bulky size. No prey can escape this excellent predator. Its victims range from tapirs and deer to capybaras and even caimans, for which it has a special liking. Jaguars and pumas are not only found in the Amazon forests but are widespread throughout the Americas. They adapt easily to most environments. In Amazonia, however, they have found optimal conditions and are the ecological counterparts of leopards and tigers of the Old World.

HUMAN INFLUENCE

Opposite page: Highway BR429 was constructed in the state of Rondonia, Brazil, to encourage colonization. From this aerial view, it looks almost like a razor cut across the thick forest cover of the Amazon. For scientists, this forest is one of the most extraordinary environments in the world. It has an immense number of plant and animal species, which up to now have remained practically unknown.

Humans appeared in South America relatively recently, having migrated through the Bering Strait. Due to a lack of sufficient archaeological evidence, it cannot be determined whether people immediately settled in Amazonia or took less difficult routes into other regions of America.

There were people occupying Amazonia about twelve thousand years ago. Very little is known about these people. Estimates of the population range from five hundred thousand to ten million. The most reasonable number is probably between two and one-half million to five million.

The principal feature of this population is how widely it was spread out. The major need of each human settlement is a wide enough territory at its disposal. The Amazonian Indians have scattered and divided into numerous tribes that differ in physical features, habits, and language. Each tribe occupies a certain territory, even though the boundaries of these areas have shifted greatly over time. A recent example is the migration of the Tupis, who left the southeastern regions of Brazil and moved toward Guyana. All of the Amazonian tribes were warlike and often divided by ferocious animosity toward their adjacent neighbors. Some believe that the wars of these tribes, together with other customs, may have had an environmental impact upon limiting population growth in the Amazonian region.

Indians and Nature

First of all, the harmonious relationship existing between the Indians and the Amazon forest must be emphasized. The natives are familiar with all of the forest resources, which they wisely classify according to a tradition passed down from generation to generation. Plants and animals, even the tiniest, have a name in all of the Indian languages, and the hunters know where to find them and how to use them. Other than the pygmy tribes of central Africa and some ethnic groups of the Indo-Pacific region, there are no better naturalists than the Amazonian Indians. Today, biologists still make use of their vast knowledge.

The Indians' primary food sources are provided, even today, by the forest. The harvest of wild plants, fruits, roots, and tubers is still important today, together with hunting and fishing. The wild resources, however, were not sufficient to sustain the populations of Amazonia. They soon took up farming, developing two distinct kinds, based on the types of soil.

In the forests of terra firma, nutrients in the soil are

Below are a quiver and blow-gun of the Yagua Indians, as well as arrow points of the Urueu-wau-wau Indians. The Yagua live in the eastern Peruvian Amazon region. The Urueu-wau-wau live in the state of Rondonia, Brazil. To the Indians, hunting is a fine art. In addition to blow-guns, they use bows and arrows with different arrow points appropriate to the game they are hunting. In many Indian tribes, however, traditional weapons have been replaced by rifles.

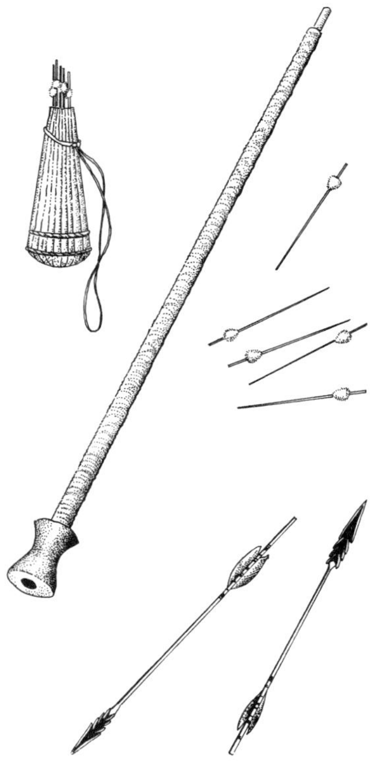

regenerated by an extremely lengthy process. The lush vegetation that grows there is fed and sustained by the minerals and salts it produces itself. For this reason, the Indians developed their practice of slash and burn agriculture. This practice is characterized by felling and burning trees to make land available for cultivation. The Indians would move every two to five years into new territories in order to give the depleted soil time to regenerate. This kind of farming is used in all tropical regions. It preserves the fertility of the ground and allows the regeneration of the forest, provided that there are not too many people and that the rotation is not too rapid. In this way, many plants were cultivated. Foremost among them was the manioc. The Indians know several varieties of this fleshy, edible, underground plant. Corn, potatoes, and other tubers were also grown, together with the fruits and spices that formed the basis of Indian cooking.

Completely different farming procedures were developed in the regions of the várzeas. There, because of annual flooding, the ground receives a constant supply of minerals and organic matter left behind when the water recedes. This precious natural fertilizer renews the productivity of the land every year. Overall, the Indians living in these regions had the same life-style as those living on terra firma. They hunted, fished (especially in the channels that were on the verge of drying up), and harvested wild plants (such as wild rice). They also cultivated many species, planting them according to the fluctuations in the water level. Of course, they had to choose the right moment and the appropriate variety so that plants would ripen before the next flooding. Manioc is well suited for this purpose, and corn can be harvested twice in between one flooding and the next.

This farming technique, based on the periodic regeneration of soils, has promoted human settlement in certain areas along the rivers. It has caused an increase in human populations, and some scientists think it created societies much more complex than those of the nomadic Indians. A rough comparison of the areas of terra firma versus those of the várzeas shows that the former comprises 98 percent of the total surface area of the Amazon, whereas the latter comprises only 2 percent. However, most of the Amazonian Indians established themselves along the rivers in the várzeas areas because of much more favorable environmental conditions found there.

A Urueu-wau-wau Indian is hunting peccaries and tapirs in the savanna. Indians also fish with bows, especially along the rapids. Arrow-fishing requires skill as well as a knowledge of the habits of aquatic animals. In pools and channels, the Indians sometimes work in pairs. One person beats the water, frightening the fish and driving them into baskets held by the second person. Sometimes the Indians pour toxic vegetable extracts into the water, which make the fish sleep.

All of the tribes identified poisons in the forests, which they used against animals and human enemies. They also discovered a variety of medicines with which they treated illnesses. At least 750 different treatments have been listed. Some cause only hallucinations, and others seem to have more psychological than therapeutic effects.

The Indians of Amazonia are perfectly suited to their environment. They know by experience all the dangers of the forest, as well as its endless resources and how to make the best use of them. When not deprived of their tribal organization they were—and still are—gracefully integrated with the world. Their beliefs, religions, and sustaining myths are all worthy of respect. They relate to the natural elements that surround them. Each of their relationships with plants and animals, and even the most ordinary of their gestures, transcends the material level. In this regard, many animals play a major role in their culture, especially the birds. The splendid ornamentations fashioned by the Indians from bird feathers, beside being beautiful, have precise sociological meanings. They are also expressive of much higher feelings.

Indian headdresses are made of feathers and down from the macaw. On the left is a Yagua headdress. On the right is the headdress of a Jvaro chief.

The First Explorers

When the first Europeans arrived in Amazonia, the region had already been touched by humans. The Indians had burned stretches of forest, which had been converted into farmland. And they had opened trails through the tangle of trees. However, the Indian populations were sparse and highly scattered, and the forest retained its original splendor.

The mouth of the Amazon River was penetrated for the first time in 1500 by a traveling companion of Christopher Columbus, Vicente Yáñez Pinzón. While he sailed along the coast in search of the route to the Indies, he was startled to suddenly find himself in a freshwater sea. He did not, however, investigate the source of the fresh waters.

In 1541, the Spanish navigator Francisco de Orellana accompanied Pizarro from Quito all the way to the eastern side of the Andes. He was seeking El Dorado, a city of fabulous riches thought by sixteenth-century explorers to exist in South America. Continuing east with his companions, he sailed up the Napo River. He reached the Amazon River and became the first explorer to enter it. He had to face almost insurmountable difficulties, including the hostility of that tribe of fierce female warriors, the Amazons.

In 1637, a Portuguese, Pedro Texeira, sailed up the Amazon all the way to Quito. He soon departed again in the opposite direction heading a large expedition. The records of these explorers formed the only documentation of then unknown lands.

In the eighteenth century, expeditions became more frequent. The first scientist to enter these regions was the Frenchman, Charles-Marie de La Condamine. He was a mathematician and astronomer, and also a lover of natural history. He had been sent to the equator for research purposes. In 1743 he decided to return to Amazonia, via the Marañón and Amazon rivers. He accumulated precious information about the hydrography (the study and description of bodies of water) of the river and the geography of the surrounding lands. He proposed the existence of a connection between the Amazon and Orinoco rivers. He also gathered information about local plants and animals. After discovering the cinchona tree and its extract, quinine, he studied the *Hevea* and its products, such as India rubber. Much later, in 1800, Alexander von Humboldt and his companion, A.J. Alexandre Bonpland, explored the Orinoco Basin, eventually entering Amazonia.

After the discovery of the vulcanization process in 1839, India rubber became a product of major importance, and some regions of Amazonia saw great economic prosperity. In the last century, latex was gathered in a cup placed at the end of a series of gashes in a rubber tree's bark. The extract was then shaped into a ball on a stick for easy transport to where it was processed.

In the last century, scientific explorations multiplied. Two Britishers played a primary role in discovering the flora and fauna of the Amazon, although they were not very well prepared for such a task. They were the land surveyor Alfred Russel Wallace and the merchant, Henry Walter Bates. Both were amateur students of natural history. In 1848 they left England and settled in Pará, today called Belém. There, they began collecting insects and other animals in order to pay for their journeys inland. Later they split up. Wallace explored the Negro River and, Bates, the Amazon and Tocantins rivers. Wallace remained in the Amazon for four years, then returned to England. From there, he went to Southeast Asia. There, he became famous and almost conceived the theory of evolution before Charles Darwin did. Bates stayed in Amazonia for eleven years, studying the flora and fauna. He discovered some biological phenomena, such as the mimicry of butterflies. These two naturalists created the solid basis for a scientific understanding of Amazonia.

Many other biologists have followed these pioneers. Today, conditions are much less taxing than in the last century. The adventure and thrill of discovery, however, remain. Thousands and thousands of species of both flora and fauna have yet to be scientifically described. In addition, many extraordinary phenomena have yet to be brought to light in this world that is, along with the oceans, the last frontier of modern times.

Colonization and Exploitation

Explorers and naturalists were soon followed by settlers and merchants ready to take immediate advantage of the real or imagined resources of Amazonia. Two towns had been founded: Pará in 1616, later called Belém, and São José de Rio Negro, later called Manaus. Others developed, scattered along the river and the coast of Guyana.

A leap in time must be made to the nineteenth century, when the India rubber fever seized Brazil and the whole world. This substance, long known to the Indians, had been little used before then. In 1839, Charles Goodyear invented vulcanization, a process that treats India rubber with chemicals to give it useful properties such as elasticity and strength. In 1888 John Dunlop patented rubber tires for vehicles, and India rubber began to be used in a many ways.

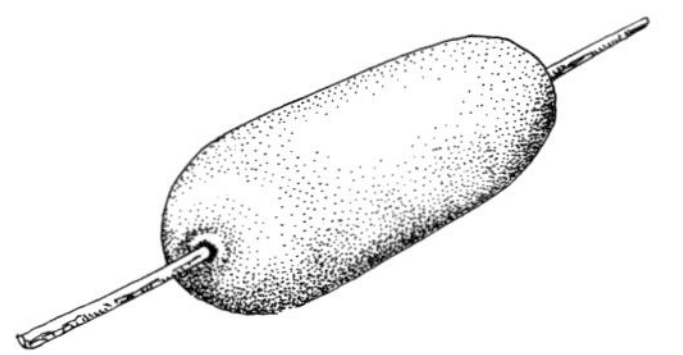

In 1866, the Emperor of Brazil opened the Amazonian harbors to international trade, but Brazilians jealously

This is an open-air gold mine in Serra Pelada, in the state of Pará, Brazil. The exploitation of the Amazon region is today undertaken by entrepreneurs, as opposed to the adventurers of past times. But the same abuses of the environment continue. Forests are destroyed and animal and plant species are threatened with extinction. In addition, the Indian farmers and workers work and live under bad conditions.

guarded their monopoly of the India rubber manufactured from *Hevea* and other latex-producing trees. In 1876, however, an Englishman, Henry Wickham, managed secretly to export seventy thousand seeds of *Hevea* from Brazil. The seeds were planted and grew in tropical Asia. In 1910, news of the first Asiatic harvests of India rubber arrived in Manaus, and the price plummeted. It was the end of the splendor of Manaus and of the boomtown frenzy for which it had become known. The thirst for India rubber would eventually cause the destruction of the Indian culture and the enslavement of both Indians and caboclos.

Latex harvesting had been conducted in the most inhumane conditions. The brutality and cruelty of the bosses, together with malnutrition and illnesses, caused the death of hundreds of thousands of Indians. Most of the illnesses, such as malaria, schistosomiasis, yellow fever, and the most deadly variety of filariasis, were spread by the settlers and by their black slaves. The Indian population is now estimated at about two hundred thousand.

Today the main resources of Amazonia are produced by plants. These are India rubber from Hevea plantations, wood for building and cabinetry, brazil nuts, vegetable oils,

The magnificent geometrical patterns of the body paint of the Waura Indians, who live in the basin of the Xingu River's upper reaches in Brazil, are displayed. At one time, the Waura supplied ceramic implements to all the other tribes and had a flourishing economy. After the introduction of metal and aluminum cookware, however, their economy was based mainly on fishing. They fish with arrows and bows, but also use barrier traps and netting. Existence of the Waura tribe, as well as that of other tribes in the area, is today seriously threatened by the construction of a highway.

fibers, palm hearts, guarana (used in making a beverage popular in Brazil), spices, and drugs. Cattle ranching on fields and tilled lands, which are turned into large *fazendas*, is a highly profitable occupation in this region. It is done, however, at great cost to forests and soil. Mineral resources in the area are also important. The Amazon is rich in manganese, lead, nickel, bauxite, copper, and large, easily accessible deposits of iron. In spite of this abundance, the large Amazonian cities are still dependent upon numerous products from around the world.

The Future of Amazonia

In the eyes of economists and politicians, this region is clearly underpopulated and underexploited. Brazil, however, faces serious development problems, since much of its territory was devastated by overexploitation and the high rate of population growth. This is especially true in the northeastern areas, which are poor and afflicted with frequent drought. For this reason there is a temptation to establish huge Amazonian business enterprises.

For the Brazilians, "The Amazon is not a problem; it is the solution," a recent slogan declares. The first stage in the utilization of the area has been the construction of roads, such as the famous trans-Amazonic highway, whose lateral branches connect it with Brasilia and with several main roads. The roads will eliminate the isolation of remote parts of the area. This has been a large and, for the most part, successful, enterprise. The second phase will include increased colonization and local development of the region. This phase will include the attraction of poor immigrants from the overpopulated northern regions, and the gradual increase in the land area allotted for farming and cattle ranching. The third phase will be the partial substitution of primeval forest with plantations of rapidly growing trees—to be used in the production of cellulose paste—and will be managed as forest reserves. This transformation would occur mainly in the regions of terra firma. The várzeas, being periodically inundated, will be embanked and turned into rice fields, or used for cultivations requiring great quantities of water.

It is certainly understandable that the countries of Amazonia, first and foremost Brazil, should try to solve their crisis and use the wide stretches of land that are presently nonproductive. However, biologists are seriously doubtful about the long-term success of these plans. They know the

A disturbing image of devastation in the Amazon forest in the state of Rondonia, Brazil is pictured. The habitats of large numbers of species are destroyed daily in this manner.

ecology of the Amazonian environment and are aware that experiments undertaken during the last decades have been costly, devastating, and unproductive. Far from being nostalgic about the past, they maintain that the present development plans for the region are founded upon a base of knowledge that is outdated. They fear the plans will seriously compromise the future of Amazonia.

The terra firma of the basin is an extremely fragile environment, not very rich in nutrients in spite of the lush forest that grows upon it. This concept must always be kept in mind. When large stretches of this land are converted into

farmland, the cycling of minerals and organic substances is interrupted. They cannot be replaced by artificial fertilizers. The overall result can be a modification of the local climate and a disruption of the water cycle.

The conversion of the várzeas into farmland, moreover, threatens to modify the cycle of high- and low-water periods. Most serious of all, this process stops the distribution of sediments that every year enrich the land flooded by water. The embankment and formation of rice fields will also gravely affect the fish population. One of the major resources of Amazonia. Fish will not be able to take advantage of food supplies from inundated forests if the embankments prohibit flooding.

It was always thought that Amazonia could become one of the granaries of the world. This is a fatal delusion. The soil is poor and fragile. Past experience should teach something. For example, whole areas around Belém have been turned into a wasteland as a result of poor farming practices. More recently, the soil of Fordlandia has been turned into a biological and agricultural desert. Finally, attempts to put to agricultural use wide stretches of land on the Jari River turned out to be a complete failure.

Amazonia is a natural treasure. It is commonly accepted that the nations that share it should try to profit from it. The problem is that, up to now, no one has been able to sustain its fertility and apparent richness over long periods. The development of these nations should not be restricted, but neither should this natural phenomenon be undervalued. The errors of the past must not be repeated. Amazonia cannot be exploited with traditional methods but should be defended and used in accordance with modern technology and knowledge. A few words must also be said for the Amazonian Indians. They are the last representatives of populations that lived for thousands of years in harmony with a sometimes hostile, but most often bountiful, nature. Modern civilization has almost completely destroyed their culture.

For many reasons, biologists wish to preserve this vast inheritance of the Amazon forests with all their plant and animal species. First of all, it is one of the most wonderful and rich environments in the world, offering subjects of study, discovery, and reflection. For the visitor, Amazonia remains a marvelous and sometimes disquieting living world. Its indispensable biological resources should remain available for both present and future generations.

GUIDE TO AREAS OF NATURAL INTEREST

Opposite page: A pirogue is crossing the Amazon forest. The mass of vegetation might give the impression that there are no animals. Actually, the forest teems with animals, but they keep hidden. Finding animals in thick forests requires an enormous amount of patience. Traveling upstream in a pirogue, one might see only a few species and then for only a fleeting moment.

Amazonia and Guyana, with their immense tropical forests and the animals that populate them, are a paradise for the naturalist. These areas are unsurpassed by any other region of the world. However, the visitor must be informed of all the difficulties inherent in observing its wildlife. It will not be an easy task. This is due to the nature of the habitat itself and to the nocturnal habits of many animals, especially the mammals. Other creatures, such as the most colorful insects and birds, never descend from the tops of the large trees. Moreover, the density of some animal populations is very low. The dangers to be encountered when visiting these areas must not be underestimated. Amazonia is a "green hell," and the anaconda, poisonous snakes, tarantulas, and jaguars, although quite dangerous, are not the primary threats. The real curses of the forest are mosquitoes, horseflies, and other biting insects that, in some periods of the year, do not give explorers any rest. Many of these insects can transmit serious illnesses. Virulent malaria, yellow fever, schistosomiasis, leishmaniasis, and other viruses and parasites are only a few of the most common of these. The water is also a vehicle for many disease-causing microbes. Only sterilized water is safe for drinking.

Without a good guide, one can easily get lost in the forests. Although the green world seems to have a lot of reference points, this is an illusion. Many explorers have left a trail only to find themselves lost in hostile forests.

Only by observing the recommended precautions can Amazonia be explored. All the same, it remains a difficult area to penetrate, probably the most difficult in the world. In order to reach the wild areas of the primeval forest and to observe the fauna, it is necessary to organize full expeditions with pirogues, rafts, guides, camping equipment, and food supplies.

Those who cannot organize such expeditions, however, have some other options. The nations sharing this huge territory have founded national parks and large reserves, some of which are open to tourists. Some of the most accessible areas are listed below. The area's animals and plants are not listed, since they are so evenly distributed in all of Amazonia. Most groups of animals are found throughout the forest, even if they are often represented in different areas by slightly varied and related species. Some parks are located in the heart of the Amazon region. Others cover more varied environments, such as the large plateaus of Guyana or the Amazonian side of the Andes.

Right: The most accessible areas of natural interest in the Amazonian states are indicated on the map. These areas are the only places to visit natural environments in Amazonia for those who do not wish to be true explorers.

Below: The area covered by Amazonian forest is indicated.

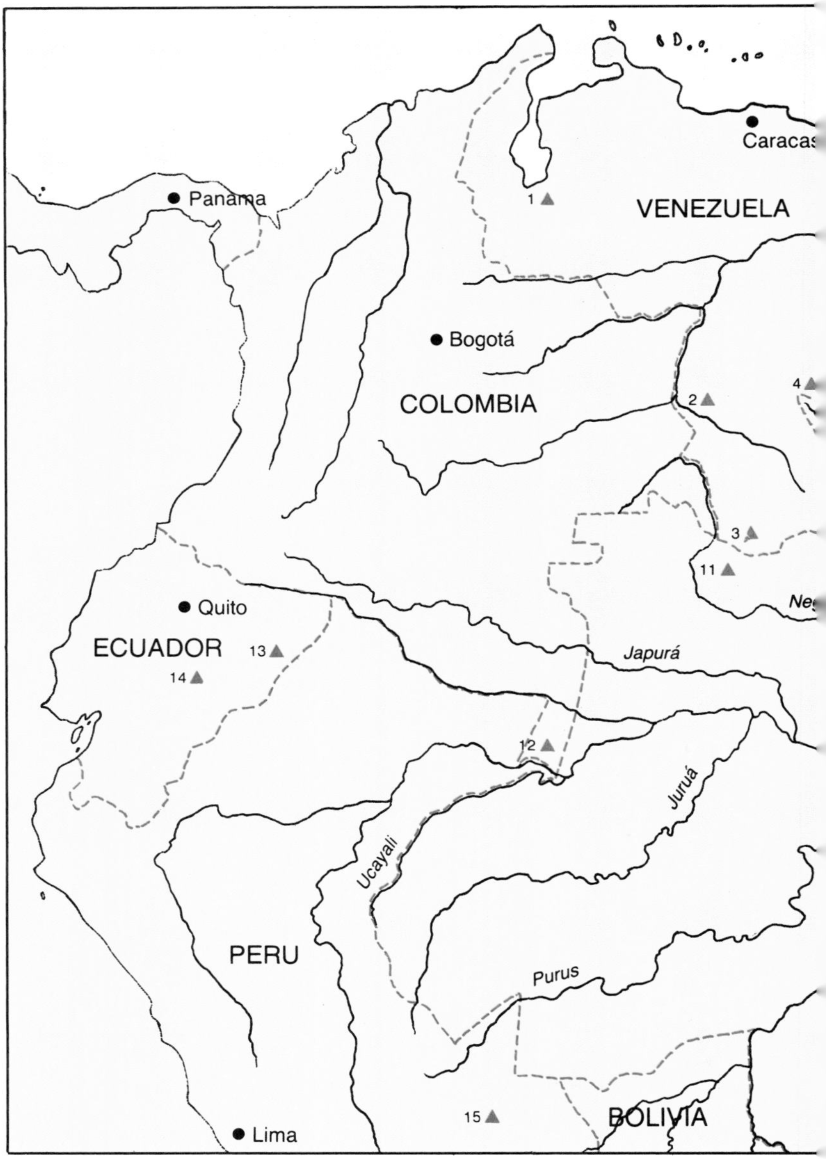

Caracas
Panama
1
VENEZUELA
Bogotá
COLOMBIA
2
4
3
11
Quito
ECUADOR
13
14
Japurá
12
Juruá
Ucayali
PERU
Purus
15
BOLIVIA
Lima

VENEZUELA

Duida-Marahuaca (1)

Founded in 1978 and comprising 810 square miles (2,100 sq. km), this national park includes some plateaus of the Roraima range and the famous Duida and Marahuaca mountains, 8,465 feet (2,580 meters high). There are spectacular landscapes crossed by tributaries of the Orinoco River. Plant species range from those of humid forests to those of savannas and mountains. Endemic species are numerous, and the fauna is widely diversified.

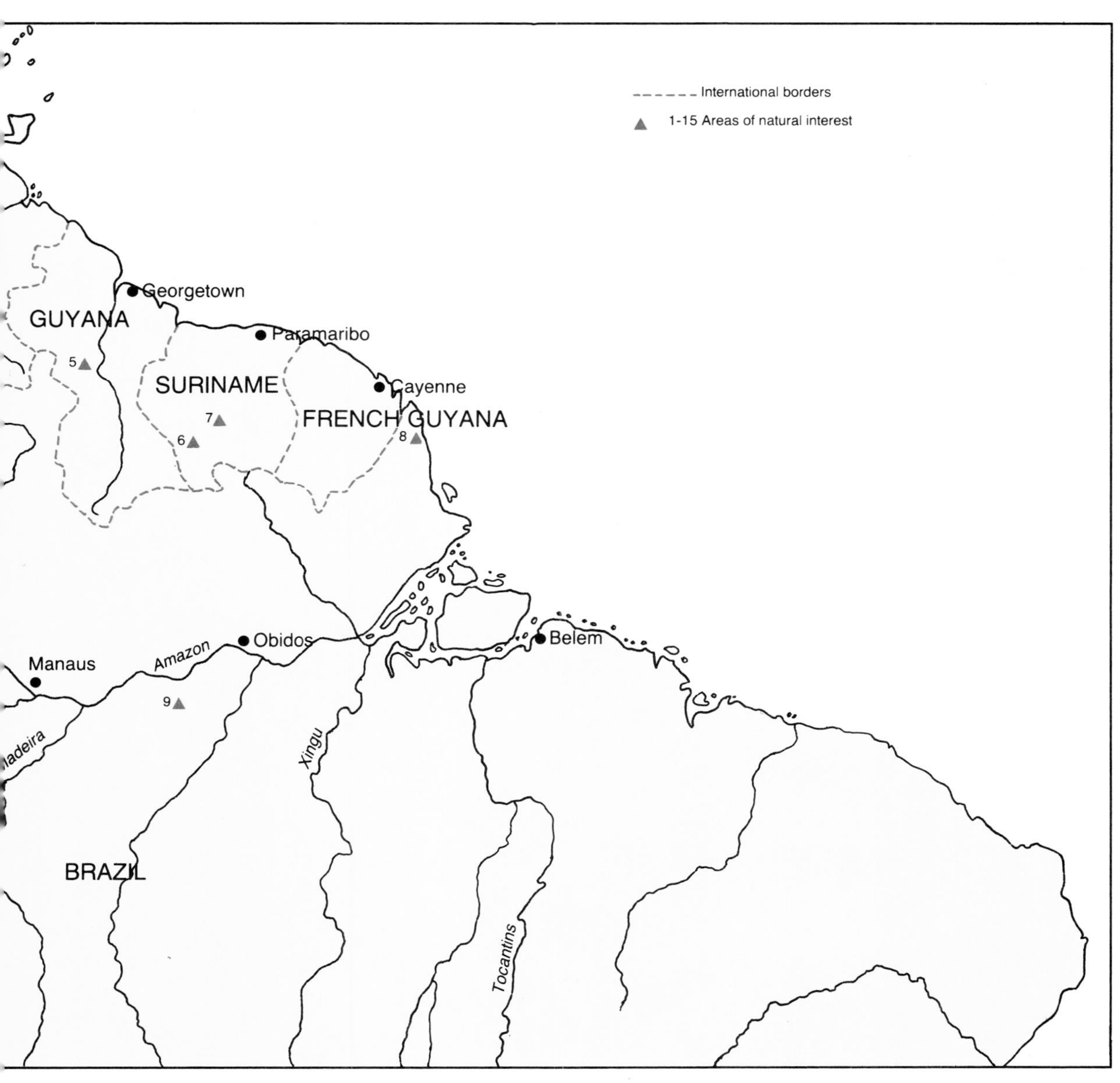

Yapacana (2)

Founded in 1978 and comprising 1,235 sq. miles (3,200 sq. km), this national park also includes some of the Roraima range. In particular, there is the Cherro Yapacana, 4,413 feet (1,345 m) high, between the Orinoco and Ventuari rivers. The plants range from those characteristic of humid forests to those found in the savannas. The plants found in this park include many species that are endemic, or native to the area.

La Neblina (3)

This national park of 5,251 sq. miles (13,600 sq. km) adjoins the national park of Pico da Neblina in Brazil. The park includes the Venezuelan side of the highest mountain (not including the Andes) in South America, the Pico da Neblina. It is 9,889 feet (3,014 m) high. It also includes the high plateaus of the Roraima range. The large variety of biological environments make the park a succession of spectacular vistas. The plants and animals are varied and include numerous endemic species.

Jaua-Sarisarinama (4)

This national park was founded in 1978 and comprises 1,274 sq. miles (3,300 sq. km). Three plateaus of the Roraima range, all geologically interesting, are also included. They provide picturesque views. The maximum altitude is around 9,800 feet (3,000 m). The park offers a great variety of plants characteristic of the humid forests of the lowlands. The rich fauna has not yet been catalogued.

GUYANA

Kaiteur (5)

Founded in 1929 as a nature reserve, this national park covers 45 sq. miles (116 sq. km). It includes stretches of flat land and deep gorges as well as the falls of Kaiteur, which are 738 feet high (225 m). In the lower elevations there are tropical, humid forests with numerous animals.

SURINAME

Eilerts de Haan Gebergte (6)
Tafelberg (7)

These two nature reserves in Suriname are very beautiful, especially Eilerts de Haan Gebergte Nature Reserve. It covers 849 sq. miles (2,200 sq. km) of humid forests and spectacular granite crests. The Tafelberg Nature Reserve, 540 sq. miles (1,400 sq. km), is a flat mountain, typical of the Guyanas. There are some humid forests. The rest of the territory is covered by dry savannas.

BRAZIL

Cabo Orange (8)

Founded in 1980, this national park has an area of 2,390 sq. miles (6,190 sq. km). It is the only federal territory in the Amapa region. It has extremely interesting, large coastal mangrove forests and a succession of lagoons, swamps, and sandy banks. Consequently, the fauna is also highly varied. The red ibis and all the animals typical of the wetlands live here. They include flamingos, sea turtles, and manatees.

Amazonia (9)

This national park stretches along on the left bank of the Tapajós River in the state of Pará. For this reason it is also called Tapajós National Park. It was founded in 1974 and has 3,860 sq. miles (10,000 sq. km). The nearby town of Santarem provides easy access to the park. Most of the area is covered by humid forest with some drier patches. The fauna is very rich, and there are also some archaeological remains.

Jau (10)

Jau was created in 1980. It is the largest national park in Brazil, having an area of 8,772 sq. miles (22,720 sq. km). It is 93 miles (150 km) northwest of Manaus, and includes rainforests with frequent palm trees, terra firma forests, and some savannas. The fauna, typical of the Amazon region, is well diversified and very rich.

Pico da Neblina (11)

Established in 1979, comprising 8,494 sq. miles (22,000 sq. km), this national park is located northeast of the state of Amazonas, between the Negro River and the Venezuelan border. The elevation ranges between 328 and 9,889 feet (100 and 3,014 m). It includes a wide variety of regions, among which is the highest mountain in Brazil, the Pico da Neblina. Together with the adjoining Venezuelan Neblina National Park, this area forms one of the largest protected regions in South America. The large variety of natural environments include humid forests, high altitude regions, and savannas of the upper reaches of the Negro River. The views, especially of the high, sheer rock, are breathtaking. Some of the savanna environments are dotted with palm groves. The species of fauna are abundant and varied.

COLOMBIA

Amacayacu (12)

The 656 sq. miles (1,700 sq. km) of this national park include stretches of low plains that lie in the valleys of the Putumayo and Amazon rivers. Created in 1975, it includes wet or flooded forests that receive abundant rainfall, evenly distributed throughout the year. The wide variety of fauna includes at least 150 species of mammals and 500 species of birds. Amphibians and reptiles are numerous, as are fish. There are also archaeological sites of major importance. The park and its surroundings are not far from the town of Leticia and are, therefore, easily accessible. The area can also be reached from Benjamin Constant, Brazil. There are organized excursions on the Cayaru River in Peru from the Isla de los Micos (Arara Lakes). This island is populated by numerous monkeys, which are easy to observe. Some Indian tribes live inland.

Following pages: A Urueu-wau-wau Indian child plays with butterflies.

ECUADOR

Yasuni (13)

Yasuni was founded in 1979 and has an area of 1,430 sq. miles (3,700 sq. km). This interesting national park extends from low regions, covered with humid forest typical of Amazonia, to the high Andean regions of the Cordillera Real at 17,717 feet (5,400 m). Consequently, the fauna is highly varied, including numerous species characteristic of the lower regions and of the hills at the foot of the Andes.

PERU

Manu (15)

Founded in 1975 and comprising an area of 5,918 sq. miles (15,328 sq. km), this national park offers visitors a great variety of natural environments. They range from the humid forests of the lower Amazonian regions to the puna typical of the Peruvian Andes. It supports numerous fauna.

GLOSSARY

adaptation: change or adjustment by which a species or individual improves its condition in relationship to its environment.

aquatic: growing or living in or upon water.

arthropod: any member of a large family of invertebrate animals with jointed legs and a segmented body.

atmosphere: the gaseous mass surrounding the earth. The atmosphere consists of oxygen, nitrogen, and other gases, and extends to a height of about 22,000 miles (35,000 km).

biology: the science that deals with the origin, history, physical characteristics, and life processes of plants and animals.

canopy: anything that covers or seems to cover, like an awning or other rooflike structure. Trees form a canopy in the forest.

carnivores: meat-eating organisms such as predatory mammals, birds of prey, or insectivorous plants.

carrion: the decaying flesh of a dead animal.

conservation: the controlled use and systematic protection of natural resources, such as forests and waterways.

continent: one of the principal land masses of the earth. Africa, Antarctica, Asia, Europe, North America, South America, and Australia are regarded as continents.

delta: a deposit of sand and soil, usually triangular in shape. Deltas are formed at the mouths of some rivers.

detritus: fragments of rock produced by disintegration or wearing away.

dominant: that species of plant or animal which is most numerous in a community, and which has control over the other organisms in its environment.

drought a prolonged period of dry weather; lack of rain.

ecology the relationship between organisms and their environment.

environment the circumstances or conditions of a plant or animal's surroundings.

epiphyte a plant, such as certain orchids or ferns, that grows on another plant upon which it depends for physical support but not for nutrients.

erosion natural processes such as weathering, abrasion, and corrosion, by which material is removed from the earth's surface. The erosive action of water is very destructive.

estuary an inlet or arm of the sea, especially the wide mouth of a river, where the tide meets the current.

evolution a gradual process in which something changes into a different and usually more complex or better form.

exotic foreign; not native; strange or different in a way that is striking or fascinating.

extinction the process of destroying or extinguishing. Many species of plant and animal life face extinction.

fauna the animals of a particular region or period.

flora the plants of a specific region or time.

fossil a remnant or trace of an organism of a past geologic age, such as a skeleton or leaf imprint, embedded in some part of the earth's crust.

geosyncline a very large, troughlike depression in the earth's surface containing masses of sedimentary and volcanic rocks.

germinate to sprout or cause to sprout or grow.

glaciers gigantic moving sheets of ice that covered great areas of the earth in an earlier time.

gregarious living in herds, flocks, or some other group.

habitat the areas or type of environment in which a person or other organism normally occurs.

hemisphere any of the halves of the earth. The earth is divided by the equator into the Northern and Southern hemispheres and by a meridian into the Eastern and Western hemispheres.

humid containing a large amount of water or water vapor.

hydrography the study, description, and mapping of oceans, lakes, and rivers, especially with reference to their navigational and commercial uses.

invertebrate lacking a backbone or spinal column.

lagoon a shallow body of water, especially one separated from the sea by sandbars or coral reefs.

larva the early, immature form of any animal that changes structurally when it becomes an adult. This process of change is called metamorphosis.

mantle the layer of the earth's interior between the crust and the core.

marsh an area of low-lying flatland, such as swamp or bog.

marsupial an animal that carries and nurses its young in a pouch on the mother's body.

metamorphosis a change in form, shape, structure, or substance as a result of development.

microclimate the climate of a small, distinct area.

migrate to move from one region to another with the change in seasons. Many animals have steady migration patterns.

mollusk an invertebrate animal characterized by a soft, usually unsegmented body, often enclosed in a shell, and having gills and a foot. Oysters, clams, and snails are mollusks.

naturalist a person who studies nature, especially by direct observation of animals and plants.

niche the specific space occupied by an organism within its habitat; a small space or hollow.

nocturnal referring to animals that are active at night.

ornithology the branch of zoology dealing with birds.

photosynthesis the process by which chlorophyll-containing cells in plants convert sunlight into chemical energy.

plumage the feathers of a bird.

precipitation water droplets or ice particles condensed from water vapor in the atmosphere, producing rain or snow that falls to the earth's surface.

transpiration the giving off of moisture through the surface of leaves and other parts of the plant.

tributary a small stream which flows into another, larger one.

vegetarian a person or animal that eats no meat, and sometimes no animal products.

vertebrate having a backbone or spinal column.

viviparous bearing or bringing forth living young.

xerophyte a plant structurally adapted to growing under very dry conditions.

zooplankton floating, often microscopic sea animals.

INDEX

	DATE DUE